PRACTICE – ASSESS – DIAGNOSE

# 180 Days of READING for First Grade

**Author**

Suzanne Barchers, Ed.D.

Shell Education

## Contributing Author

Jodene Smith, M.A.

## Publishing Credits

Dona Herweck Rice, *Editor-in-Chief*; Robin Erickson, *Production Director;* Lee Aucoin, *Creative Director;* Timothy J. Bradley, *Illustration Manager*; Conni Medina, M.A.Ed., *Editorial Director*; Sara Johnson, M.S.Ed., *Senior Editor*; Aubrie Nielsen, M.S.Ed., *Editor*; Beth Pachal, M.A.T., *Associate Education Editor*; Grace Alba, *Designer;* Alison Berry, *Illustrator*; Maple Lam, *Illustrator*; Stephanie Reid, *Photo Editor*; Corinne Burton, M.A.Ed., *Publisher*

## Image Credits

Cover, Maple Lam; p. 36, 72 Flickr; p. 60 iStock/elizabethoneillphotography.com; p.120 Flickr; p. 216 Bridgeman; all other images Shutterstock

## Standards



---

**Shell Education**
5482 Argosy Avenue
Huntington Beach, CA 92649-1030
www.tcmpub.com/shell-education

**ISBN 978-1-4258-0922-5**

# TABLE OF CONTENTS



# INTRODUCTION AND RESEARCH

## The Need for Practice

In order to be successful in today's reading classroom, students must deeply understand both concepts and procedures so that they can discuss and demonstrate their understanding. Demonstrating understanding is a process that must be continually practiced in order for students to be successful. According to Marzano, "practice has always been, and always will be, a necessary ingredient to learning procedural knowledge at a level at which students execute it independently" (2010, 83). Practice is especially important to help students apply reading comprehension strategies and word study skills.

## Understanding Assessment

In addition to providing opportunities for frequent practice, teachers must be able to assess students' comprehension and word-study skills. This is important so that teachers can adequately address students' misconceptions, build on their current understanding, and challenge them appropriately. Assessment is a long-term process that often involves careful analysis of student responses from a lesson discussion, project, practice sheet, or test. When analyzing the data, it is important for teachers to reflect on how their teaching practices may have influenced students' responses and to identify those areas where additional instruction may be required. In short, the data gathered from assessments should be used to inform instruction: slow down, speed up, or reteach. This type of assessment is called *formative assessment.*

# HOW TO USE THIS BOOK

*180 Days of Reading for First Grade* offers teachers and parents a full page of daily reading comprehension and word-study practice activities for each day of the school year.

## Easy to Use and Standards Based

These activities reinforce grade-level skills across a variety of reading concepts. The questions are provided as a full practice page, making them easy to prepare and implement as part of a classroom morning routine, at the beginning of each reading lesson, or as homework.

Every first-grade practice page provides questions that are tied to a reading or writing standard. Students are given the opportunity for regular practice in reading comprehension and word study, allowing them to build confidence through these quick standards-based activities.

| Question | College and Career Readiness Standards |
|---|---|
| | **Days 1–3** |
| 1–2 | **Reading Anchor Standard 1:** *Read closely to determine what the text says explicitly and to make logical inferences from it.* |
| 3 | **Reading Foundational Skills Standard 3:** *Know and apply grade-level phonics and word analysis skills in decoding words.* |
| 4 | **Reading Anchor Standard 4:** *Interpret words and phrases as they are used in a text, including determining technical, connotative, and figurative meanings, and analyze how specific word choices shape meaning or tone* **or**<br>**Reading Anchor Standard 6:** *Assess how point of view or purpose shapes the content and style of a text.* |
| | **Day 4** |
| 1–3 | **Reading Anchor Standard 1:** *Read closely to determine what the text says explicitly and to make logical inferences from it.* |
| 4 | **Reading Anchor Standard 2:** *Determine central ideas or themes of a text and analyze their development summarize the key supporting details and ideas.* |
| | **Day 5** |
| | **Writing Anchor Standard 4:** *Produce clear and coherent writing in which the development, organization, and style are appropriate to task, purpose, and audience.* |

# HOW TO USE THIS BOOK *(cont.)*

## Using the Practice Pages

Practice pages provide instruction and assessment opportunities for each day of the school year. The activities are organized into weekly themes, and teachers may wish to prepare packets of each week's practice pages for students. Days 1, 2, and 3 follow a consistent format, with a short piece of text and four corresponding items. As outlined on page 4, every item is aligned to a reading standard.

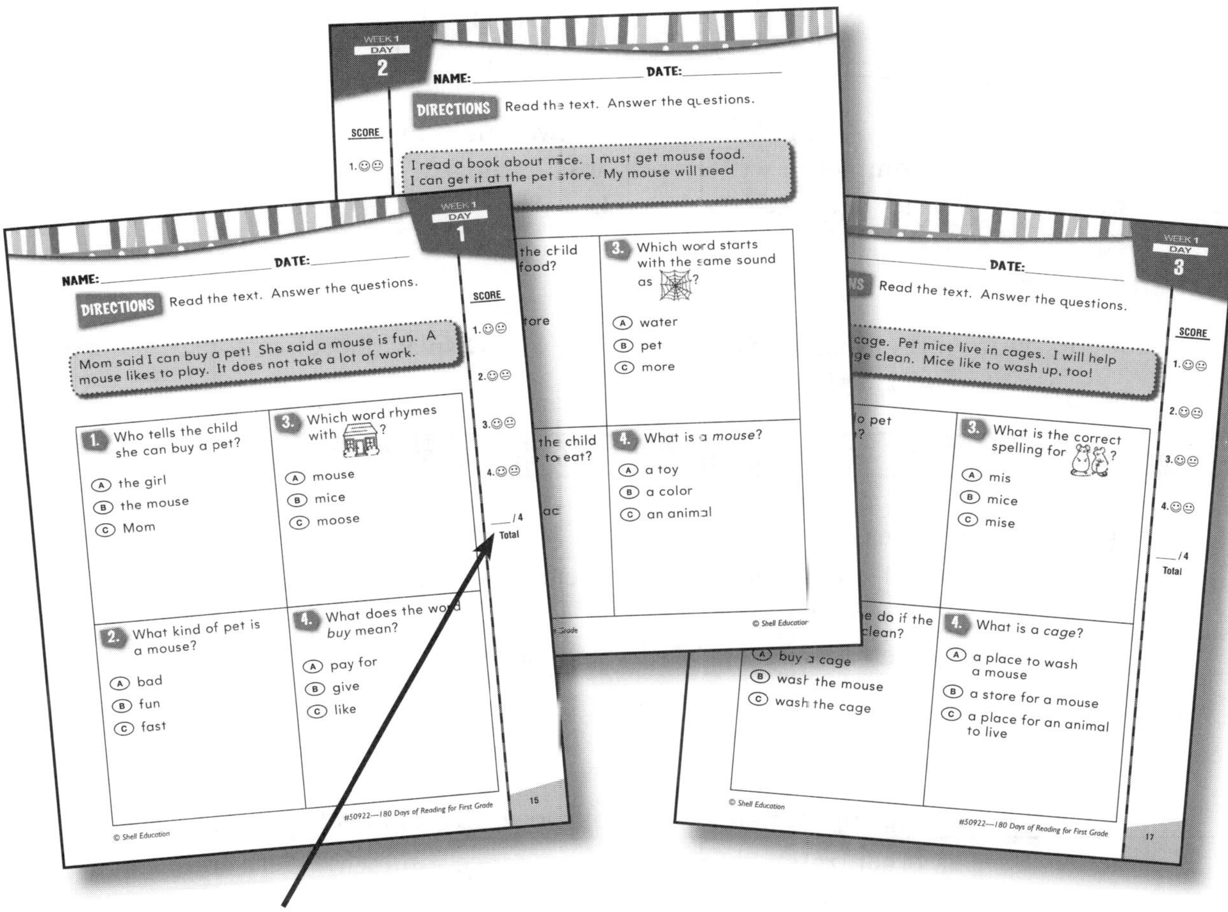


## Using the Scoring Guide

Use the scoring guide along the side of each practice page to check answers and see at a glance which skills may need more reinforcement.

Fill in the appropriate circle for each item to indicate correct (☺) or incorrect (😐) responses. You might wish to indicate only incorrect responses to focus on those skills. (For example, if students consistently miss questions 2 and 4, they may need additional help with those concepts as outlined in the table on page 4.) Use the answer key at the back of the book to score the items, or you may call out answers to have students self-score or peer-score their work.

# HOW TO USE THIS BOOK *(cont.)*

Days 4–5

NAME: DATE:

A New Home

The white mouse sat in a big cage. Then a girl said, "I want that one!" A big hand picked up the mouse and put it in a box. The mouse soon felt happy. He had a new cage and a new friend!

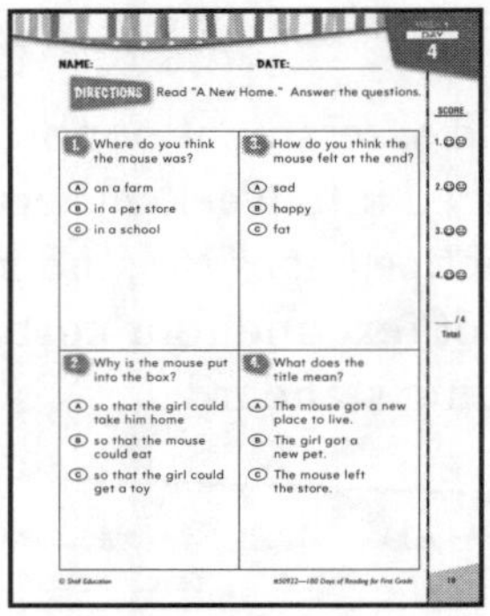
Day 4

NAME: DATE:

DIRECTIONS Read "A New Home." Answer the questions.

1. Where do you think the mouse was?
Ⓐ on a farm
Ⓑ in a pet store
Ⓒ in a school

2. Why is the mouse put into the box?
Ⓐ so that the girl could take him home
Ⓑ so that the mouse could eat
Ⓒ so that the girl could get a toy

3. How do you think the mouse felt at the end?
Ⓐ sad
Ⓑ happy
Ⓒ fat

4. What does the title mean?
Ⓐ The mouse got a new place to live.
Ⓑ The girl got a new pet.
Ⓒ The mouse left the store.

SCORE ___/4 Total

Day 5

NAME: DATE:

SCORE ___/4

Reread "A New Home."

Think about what the girl does to pick her new pet.

Write about what the girl does.

A longer text is used for Days 4 and 5. Students answer more in-depth comprehension questions on Day 4 and complete a written response to the text on Day 5. This longer text can also be used for fluency practice (see page 7).

## Writing Rubric

Score students' written response using the rubric below. Display the rubric for students to reference as they write (G1_writing_rubric.pdf).

| Points | Criteria |
|---|---|
| 4 | • Uses an appropriate organizational sequence to produce very clear and coherent writing<br>• Uses descriptive language that develops or clarifies ideas<br>• Engages the reader<br>• Uses a style very appropriate to task, purpose, and audience |
| 3 | • Uses an organizational sequence to produce clear and coherent writing<br>• Uses descriptive language that develops or clarifies ideas<br>• Engages the reader<br>• Uses a style appropriate to task, purpose, and audience |
| 2 | • Uses an organizational sequence to produce somewhat clear and coherent writing<br>• Uses some descriptive language that develops or clarifies ideas<br>• Engages the reader in some way<br>• Uses a style somewhat appropriate to task, purpose, and audience |
| 1 | • Does not use an organized sequence; the writing is not clear or coherent<br>• Uses little descriptive language to develop or clarify ideas<br>• Does not engage the reader<br>• Does not use a style appropriate to task, purpose, or audience |
| 0 | Offers no writing or does not respond to the assignment presented |

# HOW TO USE THIS BOOK *(cont.)*

## Developing Students' Fluency Skills

### What Is Fluency?

According to the National Reading Panel Report, there are five critical factors that are vital to effective reading instruction: phonemic awareness, phonics, fluency, vocabulary, and comprehension (2000). Rasinski (2006) defines fluency as "the ability to accurately and effortlessly decode the written words and then to give meaning to those words through appropriate phrasing and oral expression of the words." Wolf (2005) notes that the goal of developing fluency is comprehension rather than the ability to read rapidly. Becoming a fluent reader is a skill that develops gradually and requires practice. Reading text repeatedly with a different purpose each time supports the development of fluency in young children (Rasinski 2003).

### Assessing Fluency

Fluent readers read accurately, with expression, and at a good pace. A Fluency Rubric along with detailed instructions for scoring and keeping oral reading records is included in the digital resources (G1_fluency.pdf).

The table below lists fluency norms by grade level (Rasinski 2003):

| Student Fluency Norms Based On Words Correct Per Minute (WCPM) | | | |
|---|---|---|---|
| **Grade** | **Fall** | **Winter** | **Spring** |
| 1 | — | — | 60 wcpm |
| 2 | 53 | 78 | 94 |
| 3 | 79 | 93 | 114 |
| 4 | 99 | 112 | 118 |
| 5 | 105 | 118 | 128 |
| 6 | 115 | 132 | 145 |

# HOW TO USE THIS BOOK *(cont.)*

## Diagnostic Assessment

Teachers can use the practice pages as diagnostic assessments. The data analysis tools included with the book enable teachers or parents to quickly score students' work and monitor their progress. Teachers and parents can see at a glance which reading concepts or skills students may need to target in order to develop proficiency.

After students complete a practice page, grade each page using the answer key (pages 231–237). Then, complete the Practice Page Item Analysis for the appropriate day (pages 10–11) for the whole class, or the Student Item Analysis (pages 12–13) for individual students. These charts are also provided in the digital resources (filenames: G1_practicepage_analysis.pdf, G1_student_analysis.pdf). Teachers can input data into the electronic files directly on the computer, or they can print the pages and analyze students' work using paper and pencil.

**To complete the Practice Page Item Analyses:**

- Write or type students' names in the far-left column. Depending on the number of students, more than one copy of the form may be needed, or you may need to add rows.
- The item numbers are included across the top of the charts. Each item correlates with the matching question number from the practice page.
- For each student, record an *X* in the column if the student has the item incorrect. If the item is correct, leave the item blank.
- Count the *X*s in each row and column and fill in the correct boxes.

**To complete the Student Item Analyses:**

- Write or type the student's name on the top row. This form tracks the ongoing progress of each student, so one copy per student is necessary.
- The item numbers are included across the top of the chart. Each item correlates with the matching question number from the practice page.
- For each day, record an *X* in the column if the student has the item incorrect. If the item is correct, leave the item blank.
- Count the *X*s in each row and column and fill in the correct boxes.

# HOW TO USE THIS BOOK *(cont.)*

## Using the Results to Differentiate Instruction

Once results are gathered and analyzed, teachers can use the results to inform the way they differentiate instruction. The data can help determine which concepts are the most difficult for students and which need additional instructional support and continued practice. Depending on how often the practice pages are scored, results can be considered for instructional support on a daily or weekly basis.

## Whole-Class Support

The results of the diagnostic analysis may show that the entire class is struggling with a particular concept or group of concepts. If these concepts have been taught in the past, this indicates that further instruction or reteaching is necessary. If these concepts have not been taught in the past, this data is a great preassessment and demonstrates that students do not have a working knowledge of the concepts. Thus, careful planning for the length of the unit(s) or lesson(s) must be considered, and additional frontloading may be required.

## Small-Group or Individual Support

The results of the diagnostic analysis may show that an individual or small group of students is struggling with a particular concept or group of concepts. If these concepts have been taught in the past, this indicates that further instruction or reteaching is necessary. Consider pulling aside these students while others are working independently to instruct further on the concept(s). Teachers can also use the results to help identify individuals or groups of proficient students who are ready for enrichment or above-grade-level instruction. These students may benefit from independent learning contracts or more challenging activities. Students may also benefit from extra practice using games or computer-based resources.

## Digital Resources

Reference page 239 for information about accessing the digital resources and an overview of the contents.

# PRACTICE PAGE ITEM ANALYSIS DAYS 1–3

**Directions:** Record an *X* in cells to indicate where students have missed questions. Add up the totals. You can view the following: (1) which items were missed per student; (2) the total correct score for each student; and (3) the total number of students who missed each item.

| Week: ______ Day: ______ Item # | 1 | 2 | 3 | 4 | # correct |
|---|---|---|---|---|---|
| **Student Name** | | | | | |
| Sample Student | | X | | | 3/4 |
| | | | | | |
| | | | | | |
| | | | | | |
| | | | | | |
| | | | | | |
| | | | | | |
| | | | | | |
| | | | | | |
| | | | | | |
| | | | | | |
| | | | | | |
| | | | | | |
| | | | | | |
| | | | | | |
| | | | | | |
| | | | | | |
| **# of students missing each question** | | | | | |

# PRACTICE PAGE ITEM ANALYSIS DAYS 4–5

**Directions:** Record an *X* in cells to indicate where students have missed questions. Add up the totals. You can view the following: (1) which items were missed per student; (2) the total correct score for each student; and (3) the total number of students who missed each item.

| Week: ____ Day: ____ Item # | 1 | 2 | 3 | 4 | # correct | Written Response |
|---|---|---|---|---|---|---|
| **Student Name** | | | | | | |
| Sample Student | | X | | | 3/4 | 3 |
| | | | | | | |
| | | | | | | |
| | | | | | | |
| | | | | | | |
| | | | | | | |
| | | | | | | |
| | | | | | | |
| | | | | | | |
| | | | | | | |
| | | | | | | |
| | | | | | | |
| | | | | | | |
| | | | | | | |
| | | | | | | |
| | | | | | | |
| | | | | | | |
| **# of students missing each question** | | | | | | **Written Response Average:** |

# STUDENT ITEM ANALYSIS DAYS 1–3

**Directions:** Record an *X* in cells to indicate where the student has missed questions. Add up the totals. You can view the following: (1) which items the student missed; (2) the total correct score per day; and (3) the total number of times each item was missed.

**Student Name:** Sample Student

| **Item** | | **1** | **2** | **3** | **4** | **# correct** |
|---|---|---|---|---|---|---|
| **Week** | **Day** | | | | | |
| 1 | 1 | | X | | | 3/4 |
| | | | | | | |
| | | | | | | |
| | | | | | | |
| | | | | | | |
| | | | | | | |
| | | | | | | |
| | | | | | | |
| | | | | | | |
| | | | | | | |
| | | | | | | |
| | | | | | | |
| | | | | | | |
| | | | | | | |
| | | | | | | |
| | | | | | | |
| | | | | | | |
| | | | | | | |
| | | | | | | |
| | | | | | | |
| | | | | | | |
| **Total** | | | | | | |

 

# STUDENT ITEM ANALYSIS DAYS 4–5

**Directions:** Record an *X* in cells to indicate where the student has missed questions. Add up the totals. You can view the following: (1) which items the student missed; (2) the total correct score per day; and (3) the total number of times each item was missed.

| **Student Name:** Sample Student | | | | | | |
|---|---|---|---|---|---|---|
| | **Day 4** | | | | | **Day 5** |
| **Item** | **1** | **2** | **3** | **4** | **# correct** | **Written Response** |
| **Week** | | | | | | |
| 1 | | X | | | 3/4 | 3 |
| | | | | | | |
| | | | | | | |
| | | | | | | |
| | | | | | | |
| | | | | | | |
| | | | | | | |
| | | | | | | |
| | | | | | | |
| | | | | | | |
| | | | | | | |
| | | | | | | |
| | | | | | | |
| | | | | | | |
| | | | | | | |
| | | | | | | |
| | | | | | | |
| | | | | | | |
| **Total** | | | | | | |
| | | | | | | **Written Response Average:** |

# STANDARDS CORRELATIONS

Shell Education is committed to producing educational materials that are research and standards based. In this effort, we have correlated all of our products to the academic standards of all 50 United States, the District of Columbia, the Department of Defense Dependent Schools, and all Canadian provinces.

## How To Find Standards Correlations

To print a customized correlation report of this product for your state, visit our website at **www.tcmpub.com/shell-education** and follow the on-screen directions. If you require assistance in printing correlation reports, please contact Customer Service at 1-877-777-3450.

## Purpose and Intent of Standards

Legislation mandates that all states adopt academic standards that identify the skills students will learn in kindergarten through grade twelve. Many states also have standards for Pre-K. This same legislation sets requirements to ensure the standards are detailed and comprehensive.

Standards are designed to focus instruction and guide adoption of curricula. Standards are statements that describe the criteria necessary for students to meet specific academic goals. They define the knowledge, skills, and content students should acquire at each level. Standards are also used to develop standardized tests to evaluate students' academic progress. Teachers are required to demonstrate how their lessons meet state standards. State standards are used in the development of all of our products, so educators can be assured they meet the academic requirements of each state.

## College and Career Readiness

The activities in this book are aligned to the college and career readiness (CCR) standards. The chart on page 4 lists each standard that is addressed in this product.

## TESOL and WIDA Standards

The activities in this book promote English language development for English language learners.

**NAME:** ______________________________ **DATE:** __________________

**DIRECTIONS** Read the text. Answer the questions.

Mom said I can buy a pet! She said a mouse is fun. A mouse likes to play. It does not take a lot of work.

**1.** Who tells the child she can buy a pet?

Ⓐ the girl

Ⓑ the mouse

Ⓒ Mom

**2.** What kind of pet is a mouse?

Ⓐ bad

Ⓑ fun

Ⓒ fast

**3.** Which word rhymes with  ?

Ⓐ mouse

Ⓑ mice

Ⓒ moose

**4.** What does the word *buy* mean?

Ⓐ pay for

Ⓑ give

Ⓒ like

**SCORE**

1. ☺ ☹

2. ☺ ☹

3. ☺ ☹

4. ☺ ☹

____ / 4
**Total**

**NAME:** ____________________ **DATE:** ____________

**DIRECTIONS** Read the text. Answer the questions.

**SCORE**

1. ☺ ☹
2. ☺ ☹
3. ☺ ☹
4. ☺ ☹

____ / 4
Total

I read a book about mice. I must get mouse food. I can get it at the pet store. My mouse will need water, too.

**1.** Where can the child get mouse food?

- (A) at home
- (B) at the pet store
- (C) at a farm

**2.** What should the child give a mouse to eat?

- (A) mouse food
- (B) meat and bread
- (C) eggs

**3.** Which word starts with the same sound as ?

- (A) water
- (B) pet
- (C) more

**4.** What is a *mouse*?

- (A) a toy
- (B) a color
- (C) an animal

 

**NAME:** ____________________ **DATE:** ____________

**DIRECTIONS** Read the text. Answer the questions.

I will buy a cage. Pet mice live in cages. I will help keep the cage clean. Mice like to wash up, too!

**1.** Where do pet mice live?

Ⓐ hole

Ⓑ cage

Ⓒ cave

**2.** What will she do if the cage is not clean?

Ⓐ buy a cage

Ⓑ wash the mouse

Ⓒ wash the cage

**3.** What is the correct spelling for  ?

Ⓐ mis

Ⓑ mice

Ⓒ mise

**4.** What is a *cage*?

Ⓐ a place to wash a mouse

Ⓑ a store for a mouse

Ⓒ a place for an animal to live

**SCORE**

1. ☺ 😐

2. ☺ 😐

3. ☺ 😐

4. ☺ 😐

____ / 4 Total

**NAME:** ______________________ **DATE:** ______________

# A New Home

The white mouse sat in a big cage. Then a girl said, "I want that one!" A big hand picked up the mouse and put it in a box. The mouse soon felt happy. He had a new cage and a new friend!

**NAME:** ____________________ **DATE:** ____________

**DIRECTIONS** Read "A New Home." Answer the questions.

**SCORE**

1. ☺ ☹

2. ☺ ☹

3. ☺ ☹

4. ☺ ☹

____ / 4
Total

**1.** Where do you think the mouse was?

Ⓐ on a farm
Ⓑ in a pet store
Ⓒ in a school

**2.** Why is the mouse put into the box?

Ⓐ so that the girl could take him home
Ⓑ so that the mouse could eat
Ⓒ so that the girl could get a toy

**3.** How do you think the mouse felt at the end?

Ⓐ sad
Ⓑ happy
Ⓒ fat

**4.** What does the title mean?

Ⓐ The mouse got a new place to live.
Ⓑ The girl got a new pet.
Ⓒ The mouse left the store.

**NAME:** ______________________ **DATE:** ______________

**SCORE**

___ / 4

**Reread** "A New Home."

**Think about** what the girl does to pick her new pet.

**Write about** what the girl does.

 

**NAME:** ____________________ **DATE:** ____________

**DIRECTIONS** Read the text. Answer the questions.

**SCORE**

1. ☺ 😐
2. ☺ 😐
3. ☺ 😐
4. ☺ 😐

___ / 4
Total

Apples are good to eat. Have you seen an apple tree? You can pick your apples in the fall. That is when they are ripe.

**1.** Where do apples grow?

- (A) on a bush
- (B) on a tree
- (C) on a farm

**2.** When can you pick apples?

- (A) in the fall
- (B) in the summer
- (C) in the spring

**3.** Which word has the word *all* in it?

- (A) tree
- (B) fall
- (C) ripe

**4.** What does the word *ripe* mean?

- (A) red
- (B) older
- (C) ready

**NAME:** ____________________ **DATE:** ____________

**DIRECTIONS** Read the text. Answer the questions.

**SCORE**

1. ☺ 😐

2. ☺ 😐

3. ☺ 😐

4. ☺ 😐

___ / 4
**Total**

Cut an apple in two. The middle is called the *core*. Look at a seed. A big tree can grow from that little seed!

**1.** What do trees grow from?

Ⓐ a core
Ⓑ a seed
Ⓒ a tree

**2.** How many pieces is the apple cut into?

Ⓐ It is not cut.
Ⓑ three
Ⓒ two

**3.** Which word rhymes with  ?

Ⓐ core
Ⓑ apple
Ⓒ seed

**4.** What is the middle of an apple called?

Ⓐ a stem
Ⓑ a seed
Ⓒ a core

 

**NAME:** ______________________ **DATE:** ______________

**DIRECTIONS** Read the text. Answer the questions.

SCORE

1. ☺ 😐

2. ☺ 😐

3. ☺ 😐

4. ☺ 😐

___ / 4
Total

You can eat an apple. You also can make applesauce. Apples can be made into juice. But an apple pie is best!

**1.** What are some ways to eat apples?

Ⓐ in a sauce or in a pan

Ⓑ as juice or in a glass

Ⓒ as juice or as sauce

**2.** What does the writer like best?

Ⓐ apple juice

Ⓑ apple pie

Ⓒ raw apples

**3.** Which word is made up of two words?

Ⓐ apple

Ⓑ into

Ⓒ best

**4.** What is an ***apple***?

Ⓐ a fruit

Ⓑ a season

Ⓒ a drink

**NAME:** ______________________ **DATE:** ______________

# Bobbing for Apples

Get ready for a fun game! This is what to do. First, get a big tub. Put water in the tub. Add lots of apples. Take turns with some friends. Try to get an apple out. No hands! You have to bite your apple. Have fun bobbing for apples!

**NAME:** ______________________ **DATE:** ______________

**DIRECTIONS** Read "Bobbing for Apples." Answer the questions.

**SCORE**

1. ☺ ☹
2. ☺ ☹
3. ☺ ☹
4. ☺ ☹

____ / 4
Total

**1.** What might happen in the game?

Ⓐ You might get wet.

Ⓑ You might eat a lot.

Ⓒ You might make a pie.

**2.** What do you need for this game?

Ⓐ water, a big tub, and a mop

Ⓑ water, little pans, and apples

Ⓒ water, a big tub, and apples

**3.** What does the word *bobbing* mean?

Ⓐ eating

Ⓑ moving your head up and down

Ⓒ jumping

**4.** What is the main idea?

Ⓐ how to play the game

Ⓑ how to clean apples

Ⓒ how to fill a tub

NAME: ______________________ DATE: ______________

SCORE

___ / 4

**Reread** "Bobbing for Apples."

**Think about** how to bob for apples.

**Write about** how to play the game.

 

NAME: ______________________ DATE: ________________

**DIRECTIONS** Read the text. Answer the questions.

SCORE

1. ☺ 😐

2. ☺ 😐

3. ☺ 😐

4. ☺ 😐

____ / 4
Total

The leaves are red and gold. It is cool at night. Orange pumpkins are in the stores. Fall is here at last!

**1.** What time of year is it in the text?

Ⓐ spring

Ⓑ fall

Ⓒ summer

**2.** What colors are the leaves?

Ⓐ green and yellow

Ⓑ green and orange

Ⓒ red and gold

**3.** Which word starts with the same sound as ?

Ⓐ gold

Ⓑ pumpkin

Ⓒ can

**4.** What does the word *cool* mean?

Ⓐ a little cold

Ⓑ a little windy

Ⓒ a little warm

**NAME:** ______________________ **DATE:** ______________

**DIRECTIONS** Read the text. Answer the questions.

SCORE

1. ☺ 😐

2. ☺ 😐

3. ☺ 😐

4. ☺ 😐

___ / 4
Total

Are there leaves on the ground? Get a rake and get to work. Make a great big leaf pile. Jump in! It is fun!

**1.** Where does this text take place?

Ⓐ outside

Ⓑ inside

Ⓒ on a farm

**2.** What can you do with a rake?

Ⓐ trim a tree

Ⓑ pile up leaves

Ⓒ get a job

**3.** Which is the correct spelling for  ?

Ⓐ rak

Ⓑ rakk

Ⓒ rake

**4.** What does *it* refer to in the text?

Ⓐ the leaves falling on the ground

Ⓑ jumping in the pile of leaves

Ⓒ raking the leaves

 

**NAME:** ____________________ **DATE:** ____________

**DIRECTIONS** Read the text. Answer the questions.

Football is fun in the fall. You can watch a game on TV. Do you like to run or kick? You may want to play, too!

**1.** When are football games fun?

(A) in the fall

(B) in the morning

(C) in the summer

**2.** What is a football?

(A) a kind of foot

(B) a kind of game

(C) a kind of shoe

**3.** Which two words make ?

(A) *base* and *ball*

(B) *basket* and *ball*

(C) *foot* and *ball*

**4.** What does the word *kick* mean?

(A) to hit with your foot

(B) to hit with your leg

(C) to hit with your arm

**SCORE**

1. ☺ ☹

2. ☺ ☹

3. ☺ ☹

4. ☺ ☹

____ / 4 Total

NAME: ______________________ DATE: ______________

# Two Falls

The leaves were bright last fall. There were sunny days and cool nights. The sun helps the leaves make food. This helps the leaves keep their colors. This year, the nights are warm and the days are cool. There are lots of clouds. The leaves are dull. But I still love fall!

NAME: ______________________ DATE: ______________

**DIRECTIONS** Read "Two Falls." Answer the questions.

**1.** Why were the leaves bright last fall?

(A) There was a lot of rain.

(B) The leaves were red and gold.

(C) The leaves could make food.

**2.** What is the weather like this year?

(A) warm nights and cool days

(B) cloudy days and cool nights

(C) warm nights and sunny days

**3.** What does the text tell you about leaves?

(A) that they grow on trees

(B) that they need sun to make their food

(C) that they need clouds to stay bright

**4.** What is the main idea?

(A) Leaves are bright or dull.

(B) Leaves change in the fall.

(C) Clouds make leaves dull.

**SCORE**

1. ☺ 😐

2. ☺ 😐

3. ☺ 😐

4. ☺ 😐

____ / 4 Total

**NAME:** ______________________ **DATE:** ______________

SCORE

___/4

**Reread** "Two Falls."

**Think about** whether the leaves change color in the fall where you live.

**Write about** what fall is like where you live.

**NAME:** ____________________ **DATE:** ______________

**DIRECTIONS** Read the text. Answer the questions.

Ants have a queen just like bees do. Her job is to lay the eggs. All the other ants work for her.

**1.** How are ants and bees alike?

(A) They both like honey.

(B) They live in the same place.

(C) They both have a queen.

**2.** What does the queen do?

(A) She makes the ants work.

(B) She lays the eggs.

(C) She gets the food.

**3.** Which picture rhymes with *ants*?

(A) 

(B) 

(C) 

**4.** Who does *her* refer to in this text?

(A) the queen

(B) the ants

(C) a girl

**SCORE**

1.

2.

3.

4.

___ / 4

Total

**NAME:** ______________________ **DATE:** ______________

**DIRECTIONS** Read the text. Answer the questions.

**SCORE**

1. ☺ 😐
2. ☺ 😐
3. ☺ 😐
4. ☺ 😐

___ / 4
Total

Some worker ants look for food. They use smell to mark a trail to the food. Then more ants can find the food.

**1.** A worker ant finds food. What happens next?

Ⓐ More ants can find the food. The ants use smell to mark a trail to the food.

Ⓑ More ants look for food.

Ⓒ Ants stay in the nest.

**2.** How do ants use smell?

Ⓐ to find the way home

Ⓑ to tell if the food is good

Ⓒ to tell other ants where food is

**3.** Which word ends with the same sound as ?

Ⓐ food

Ⓑ mark

Ⓒ ant

**4.** What does the word *ants* mean?

Ⓐ one ant

Ⓑ zero ants

Ⓒ many ants

**NAME:** ______________________ **DATE:** ______________

**DIRECTIONS** Read the text. Answer the questions.

**SCORE**

1. ☺ 😐
2. ☺ 😐
3. ☺ 😐
4. ☺ 😐

____ / 4
Total

Have you had an ant bite? Some ants will bite or sting to stay safe. Most ants just want to do their jobs.

**1.** Why do some ants bite?

Ⓐ to get food
Ⓑ to get to the nest
Ⓒ to stay safe

**2.** What do most ants want to do?

Ⓐ work
Ⓑ sting
Ⓒ bite

**3.** Which word has the same vowel sound as ?

Ⓐ sting
Ⓑ bite
Ⓒ their

**4.** What is the opposite of *safe*?

Ⓐ hurt
Ⓑ not hurt
Ⓒ bit

NAME: ______________________ DATE: ______________

# The Ant Farm

Get an ant farm if you want to learn a lot about ants. You can see how strong ants are. You can watch them make tunnels and eat. Your ants will be fun to watch. But you have to take care of them, too.

**NAME:** ______________________ **DATE:** ______________

**DIRECTIONS** Read "The Ant Farm." Answer the questions.

**SCORE**

1. ☺ 😐
2. ☺ 😐
3. ☺ 😐
4. ☺ 😐

____ / 4
Total

**1.** What is an ant farm?

Ⓐ a container for ants to live in

Ⓑ a farm to grow ant food

Ⓒ a hole outside where ants live

**2.** What are ant farms good for?

Ⓐ to learn how to farm

Ⓑ to get a new pet

Ⓒ to learn how ants work

**3.** Think about ant farms. Which is true?

Ⓐ Ants do not work much.

Ⓑ Ants make tunnels.

Ⓒ An ant farm has a farmer.

**4.** What does this text tell you?

Ⓐ how to find ants

Ⓑ what an ant farm is

Ⓒ how to watch ants

**NAME:** ____________________ **DATE:** ____________

SCORE
___/ 4

**Reread** "The Ant Farm."

**Think about** whether ants should be in their nests or in an ant farm.

**Write about** whether you think ant farms are good or bad.

 

**NAME:** ____________________ **DATE:** ______________

**DIRECTIONS** Read the text. Answer the questions.

> Dad and Pam want to cook a pumpkin. First, Dad cuts it open. Then, they clean it out. They wash the seeds.

**1.** Who cuts the pumpkin?

Ⓐ Pam
Ⓑ Dad
Ⓒ the seeds

**2.** What do Pam and Dad do with the seeds?

Ⓐ wash them
Ⓑ eat them
Ⓒ toss them away

**3.** Which word rhymes with ?

Ⓐ cook
Ⓑ seed
Ⓒ open

**4.** Which sentence uses the word *cut* in the same way as in the text?

Ⓐ I saw someone cut in line.
Ⓑ Cut the pizza.
Ⓒ We cut through the park to get home.

**SCORE**

1. ☺ 😐
2. ☺ 😐
3. ☺ 😐
4. ☺ 😐

____ / 4
Total

NAME: ____________________ DATE: ____________

**DIRECTIONS** Read the text. Answer the questions.

SCORE

1. ☺ 😐

2. ☺ 😐

3. ☺ 😐

4. ☺ 😐

____ / 4
Total

Dad puts oil in a pan. Pam adds the pumpkin seeds. Dad adds a bit of salt. Time to bake the seeds!

**1.** Who puts things in the pan?

(A) Pam
(B) oil and salt
(C) Pam and Dad

**2.** What are Pam and Dad doing?

(A) cleaning the pumpkin
(B) baking the seeds
(C) making a pie

**3.** Which word has the same vowel sound as *seeds*?

(A) clean
(B) bake
(C) step

**4.** Which sentence uses the word *bit* in the same way as the text?

(A) The dog bit the boy.
(B) Put the bit in the horse's mouth.
(C) Only use a little bit of glue.

 

**NAME:** ______________________________ **DATE:** __________________

**DIRECTIONS** Read the text. Answer the questions.

Dad cuts up the pumpkin. Pam peels it. They put the pieces into a pot. They let it boil. Then they mash it.

**1.** Where are Dad and Pam?

- Ⓐ in a kitchen
- Ⓑ in a pumpkin patch
- Ⓒ in a store

**2.** What do they do last?

- Ⓐ boil the pumpkin
- Ⓑ mash the pumpkin
- Ⓒ peel the pumpkin

**3.** Which is the correct spelling for  ?

- Ⓐ punkin
- Ⓑ pumpkin
- Ⓒ pumcan

**4.** What does the word *it* refer to in this text?

- Ⓐ Dad
- Ⓑ the pot
- Ⓒ the pumpkin

**SCORE**

1. ☺ 😐
2. ☺ 😐
3. ☺ 😐
4. ☺ 😐

____ / 4 Total

**NAME:**____________________________ **DATE:**________________

# The Pumpkin Surprise

Pam and Dad make a pie crust. They make the pie filling. They fill the crust. But there is still more pumpkin left! They make pumpkin cookies. There is still more pumpkin left! Dad said, "We can use it for breakfast!"

NAME: ______________________ DATE: ______________

**DIRECTIONS** Read "The Pumpkin Surprise." Answer the questions.

SCORE

1. ☺ 😐
2. ☺ 😐
3. ☺ 😐
4. ☺ 😐

____ / 4
Total

**1.** Why do Pam and Dad make cookies?

Ⓐ They like cookies.

Ⓑ They had more pumpkin.

Ⓒ They had more pie crust.

**2.** Why do they have so much pumpkin?

Ⓐ The pumpkin is very big.

Ⓑ The pumpkin has lots of seeds.

Ⓒ They like to fix pumpkin.

**3.** What do you think Dad will make for breakfast?

Ⓐ pumpkin pancakes

Ⓑ more pumpkin pie

Ⓒ eggs and toast

**4.** What is the main idea of the text?

Ⓐ Pam and Dad like to make pie.

Ⓑ Pam and Dad use a lot of pumpkin.

Ⓒ Pam and Dad will not make pie again.

**NAME:** ______________________ **DATE:** ______________

SCORE

___ / 4

**Reread** "The Pumpkin Surprise."

**Think about** the big mess Pam and Dad made.

**Write about** what Pam and Dad do next.

 

**NAME:** ____________________ **DATE:** ______________

**DIRECTIONS** Read the text. Answer the questions.

Would you eat ten packs of sugar? A can of soda may have that much sugar. The best drink for your body is water.

**1.** Which is true?

(A) Sugar is good for you.
(B) Water has sugar in it.
(C) Water is good for you.

**2.** How much sugar may a can of soda have?

(A) a cup
(B) ten packets
(C) two cups

**3.** Which word starts with the same sound as *sugar*?

(A) shop
(B) such
(C) sun

**4.** What is *sugar*?

(A) a sweet powder
(B) a drink
(C) water

**SCORE**

1. ☺ ☹
2. ☺ ☹
3. ☺ ☹
4. ☺ ☹

____ / 4
Total

**NAME:** ______________________ **DATE:** ______________

**DIRECTIONS** Read the text. Answer the questions.

SCORE

1. ☺ 😐

2. ☺ 😐

3. ☺ 😐

4. ☺ 😐

____ / 4
Total

Do you like a snack after school? Skip the cookies. Eat some fruit. Put peanut butter on celery sticks. You will feel good!

**1.** Which makes a good snack?

Ⓐ healthy foods
Ⓑ anything you want
Ⓒ fast food

**2.** Which snack is **not** good for you?

Ⓐ peanut butter on apple slices
Ⓑ cookies and soda
Ⓒ apple slices and bananas

**3.** Which word rhymes with  ?

Ⓐ school
Ⓑ snack
Ⓒ bricks

**4.** Which is a fruit?

Ⓐ banana
Ⓑ carrot
Ⓒ peanut butter

 

**NAME:** ______________________ **DATE:** ______________

**DIRECTIONS** Read the text. Answer the questions.

Do you like salad for lunch? Some schools have a salad bar. Some have fruit, too. Schools want to have good foods that children like.

**1.** What do some schools have for lunch?

Ⓐ soup and a sandwich bar

Ⓑ fruit and a salad bar

Ⓒ pizza and potato chips

**2.** Why do schools want to have good foods?

Ⓐ so children will play a lot

Ⓑ so children will eat good foods

Ⓒ so children will like it

**3.** Which word has the same vowel sound as  ?

Ⓐ salad

Ⓑ fruit

Ⓒ lunch

**4.** What is *lunch*?

Ⓐ the meal eaten in the morning

Ⓑ the meal eaten in the middle of the day

Ⓒ the meal eaten in the evening

**SCORE**

1. ☺ 😐

2. ☺ 😐

3. ☺ 😐

4. ☺ 😐

____ / 4

**Total**

**NAME:** ______________________ **DATE:** ______________

# School Lunch in France

Schools in France want children to eat good lunches. Most kids like ketchup. But ketchup has a lot of sugar. Children in France can have ketchup just once a week. That is when kids get to eat a burger and French fries.

NAME: ______________________ DATE: ________________

**DIRECTIONS** Read "School Lunch in France." Answer the questions.

**SCORE**

1. ☺ 😐
2. ☺ 😐
3. ☺ 😐
4. ☺ 😐

____ / 4
Total

**1.** Why do schools in France want good lunches for children?

Ⓐ so they will eat ketchup

Ⓑ so they will eat healthy

Ⓒ so they will eat burgers

**2.** What do children eat with ketchup?

Ⓐ french fries

Ⓑ pickles

Ⓒ sugar

**3.** What is the problem with ketchup?

Ⓐ It tastes bad.

Ⓑ It costs a lot.

Ⓒ It has a lot of sugar.

**4.** What is the main idea?

Ⓐ Children in France don't like ketchup.

Ⓑ Schools in France give out less ketchup.

Ⓒ Schools in France don't like children.

**NAME:** ______________________ **DATE:** ______________

SCORE
___ /4

**Reread** "School Lunch in France."

**Think about** the lunches children eat in France and the lunches you eat.

**Write about** what you think the best school lunch is.

 

**NAME:** ____________________ **DATE:** ______________

**DIRECTIONS** Read the text. Answer the questions.

**SCORE**

1. ☺ 😐
2. ☺ 😐
3. ☺ 😐
4. ☺ 😐

___ / 4
Total

Mark and Pam love to dress up. They also like to make their costumes. "We should have a parade!" says Mark.

**1.** What do Mark and Pam like to do?

Ⓐ go on hikes
Ⓑ dress up
Ⓒ take naps

**2.** What kind of parade will they have?

Ⓐ circus
Ⓑ singing
Ⓒ costume

**3.** Which word does **not** end with the same sound as  ?

Ⓐ dress
Ⓑ make
Ⓒ mark

**4.** Who does *they* refer to in this text?

Ⓐ the parade
Ⓑ Mark and Pam
Ⓒ the costumes

**NAME:** ______________________ **DATE:** ______________

**DIRECTIONS** Read the text. Answer the questions.

SCORE

1. ☺😐

2. ☺😐

3. ☺😐

4. ☺😐

___ / 4
Total

Mark and Pam ask Kim and Lee to help. They bring their dogs along. Mark says, "We can have a pet parade instead!"

**1.** Who helps Mark and Pam?

Ⓐ the dogs
Ⓑ the parade
Ⓒ Kim and Lee

**2.** What does Mark want to do?

Ⓐ have a snack
Ⓑ make pet houses
Ⓒ have a pet parade

**3.** Which word does **not** rhyme with *bring*?

Ⓐ ring
Ⓑ dog
Ⓒ sing

**4.** Who does *we* refer to in this text?

Ⓐ all the children
Ⓑ Kim and Lee
Ⓒ Mark and Pam

 

**NAME:** ______________________ **DATE:** ______________

**DIRECTIONS** Read the text. Answer the questions.

**SCORE**

1. ☺ 😐

2. ☺ 😐

3. ☺ 😐

4. ☺ 😐

___ / 4
Total

Lee puts a cowboy hat on his dog. Kim dresses her dog in a clown hat and skirt. Pam puts bunny ears on her cat. Mark puts his cat in a stroller.

**1.** Who gets dressed up?

Ⓐ Lee
Ⓑ the pets
Ⓒ Pam

**2.** Which pet is dressed like a rabbit?

Ⓐ Lee's dog
Ⓑ Kim's dog
Ⓒ Pam's cat

**3.** The word *cowboy* is made of two words: *cow* and *boy*. Which word is made of two words?

Ⓐ baseball
Ⓑ balloon
Ⓒ flower

**4.** What does the word *dresses* mean in this text?

Ⓐ puts clothing on
Ⓑ a type of clothing
Ⓒ a dog in a dress

**NAME:** ______________________ **DATE:** ______________

# The Pet Parade

The parade starts at noon. More children bring pets in costumes. One dog looks like a bee. A puppy wears a crown. A cat rides like a baby in a stroller. The pets do not look happy. But then the dogs get dog treats. The cats get toys. Now they are all happy!

**NAME:** ______________________ **DATE:** ______________

**DIRECTIONS** Read "The Pet Parade." Answer the questions.

**SCORE**

1. ☺ 😐
2. ☺ 😐
3. ☺ 😐
4. ☺ 😐

____ / 4
Total

**1.** How do you think the children feel about the parade?

Ⓐ hungry
Ⓑ tired
Ⓒ happy

**2.** What is in the stroller?

Ⓐ a baby
Ⓑ a cat
Ⓒ a dog

**3.** Why do you think the pets were unhappy?

Ⓐ They did not like being in costumes.
Ⓑ They wanted to go home.
Ⓒ They did not like the other pets.

**4.** What is another good title for this text?

Ⓐ Making Pets Happy
Ⓑ Pets at Halloween
Ⓒ Animals on Parade

**NAME:** ______________________ **DATE:** ______________

**SCORE**

___ / 4

**Reread** "The Pet Parade."

**Think about** how you would dress a pet for a parade.

**Write about** what your pet parade would be like.

 

**NAME:** ______________________ **DATE:** ______________

**DIRECTIONS** Read the text. Answer the questions.

Firefighters live at the fire station on work days. They stay there to be ready to help fight fires. Fire! It is time to get on the truck!

**1.** Where do firefighters live on work days?

- (A) at home
- (B) at the fire station
- (C) on the fire truck

**2.** Why do firefighters live at the station?

- (A) to be ready when there is a fire
- (B) to help put out a fire
- (C) to learn how to put out a fire

**3.** Which is the correct spelling for  ?

- (A) truk
- (B) truke
- (C) truck

**4.** What is a *station*?

- (A) a place that gives a service
- (B) a food that firefighters eat
- (C) a fire in a place that sells gas

**SCORE**

1. ☺ 😐

2. ☺ 😐

3. ☺ 😐

4. ☺ 😐

___ / 4
Total

**NAME:** ______________________ **DATE:** ______________

**DIRECTIONS** Read the text. Answer the questions.

**SCORE**

1. ☺ ☹

2. ☺ ☹

3. ☺ ☹

4. ☺ ☹

____ / 4
**Total**

A fire truck does a big job. It takes the firefighters to the fire. It also takes tools, like the hose and an ax.

**1.** What is the fire truck's job?

Ⓐ to start the fire

Ⓑ to take firefighters and tools to the fire

Ⓒ to put out the fire

**2.** Which might you find on a fire truck?

Ⓐ 

Ⓑ 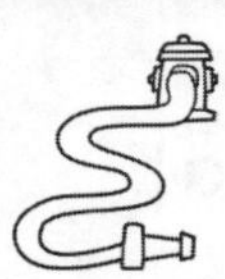

Ⓒ 

**3.** Which word has the same middle sound as ?

Ⓐ tool

Ⓑ hose

Ⓒ goes

**4.** How many does the word *tools* mean?

Ⓐ one

Ⓑ none

Ⓒ more than one

 

**NAME:** ______________________ **DATE:** ______________

**DIRECTIONS** Read the text. Answer the questions.

Have you ever played with a toy fire truck? Some kids have metal or plastic trucks. Others have trucks made out of wood. Is there a fire? Let's pretend!

**1.** What can toy fire trucks be made out of?

Ⓐ metal, plastic, or wood

Ⓑ rubber

Ⓒ wood and fire

**2.** What can you do with a toy fire truck?

Ⓐ pretend there is a fire

Ⓑ put out a real fire

Ⓒ make a fire truck

**3.** Which word rhymes with *truck*?

Ⓐ train

Ⓑ duck

Ⓒ kick

**4.** Which sentence uses the word *played* in the same way as the text?

Ⓐ The girls played in the yard.

Ⓑ She played a frog in the play.

Ⓒ He played the card on his turn.

**SCORE**

1. ☺ 😐

2. ☺ 😐

3. ☺ 😐

4. ☺ 😐

___ / 4
Total

**NAME:** ______________________ **DATE:** ____________

# Fire Dog

They call me Spot. I live with the firefighters. I do not get to ride on the fire truck. I will stay at the station. I will watch over things. I like it best when we are all home.

**NAME:** ____________________ **DATE:** ____________

**DIRECTIONS** Read "Fire Dog." Answer the questions.

1. Why do you think the dog is called Spot?

Ⓐ He has black spots.

Ⓑ He is black and white.

Ⓒ He has a helmet.

2. Where does Spot live?

Ⓐ Spot lives on the fire truck.

Ⓑ Spot lives in a home.

Ⓒ Spot lives at a fire station.

3. What does Spot like best?

Ⓐ when he watches the fire station

Ⓑ when they are all at the fire station

Ⓒ when they have dinner

4. What is another good title for this text?

Ⓐ Taking a Ride

Ⓑ Why Dogs Have Spots

Ⓒ The Firehouse Dog

**SCORE**

1. ☺ 😐

2. ☺ 😐

3. ☺ 😐

4. ☺ 😐

____ / 4
**Total**

**NAME:** ______________________ **DATE:** ______________

SCORE

___ / 4

**Reread** "Fire Dog."

**Think about** what Spot does at work every day. What will he do? What will he eat?

**Write about** the next day at work for Spot.

 

**NAME:** ______________________ **DATE:** ______________

**DIRECTIONS** Read the text. Answer the questions.

**SCORE**

1. ☺ 😐
2. ☺ 😐
3. ☺ 😐
4. ☺ 😐

____ / 4
Total

Jon and Mark go to the city. First, they walk to the subway. They buy tickets. Then they wait ten minutes for the subway.

**1.** Where are Jon and Mark going?

Ⓐ to the city

Ⓑ to town

Ⓒ for a ride

**2.** Why do they have to wait?

Ⓐ for the subway train to come

Ⓑ for a friend to come

Ⓒ to eat a snack

**3.** The word *subway* is made of two words: *sub* and *way*. Which word is made of two words?

Ⓐ happy

Ⓑ garden

Ⓒ without

**4.** Who does *they* refer to in this text?

Ⓐ the subway

Ⓑ the tickets

Ⓒ Jon and Mark

NAME: ______________________ DATE: ______________

**DIRECTIONS** Read the text. Answer the questions.

SCORE

1. ☺ 😐

2. ☺ 😐

3. ☺ 😐

4. ☺ 😐

____ / 4
Total

The subway train comes right on time. Jon and Mark get on the train. It is full of riders. They hold on to a pole.

**1.** Who rides the subway?

Ⓐ the train
Ⓑ the pole
Ⓒ Mark and Jon

**2.** Why do Jon and Mark stand?

Ⓐ There are no seats.
Ⓑ They like standing.
Ⓒ They are late.

**3.** Which word rhymes with *right*?

Ⓐ first
Ⓑ bite
Ⓒ high

**4.** What does the word *riders* mean?

Ⓐ people who take a walk
Ⓑ people who take a ride
Ⓒ one person who takes a ride

**NAME:** ____________________ **DATE:** ______________

**DIRECTIONS** Read the text. Answer the questions.

The streets are very busy. Cars and trucks rush by. Jon and Mark walk a lot to get places. They pass lots of stores on their way.

**1.** Where are Jon and Mark walking?

Ⓐ in the subway

Ⓑ in the city

Ⓒ in the countryside

**2.** Why do you think they walk a lot?

Ⓐ They are looking for the subway.

Ⓑ They are going someplace.

Ⓒ They are lost and hungry.

**3.** Which picture ends with the same sound as *rush*?

Ⓐ 

Ⓑ 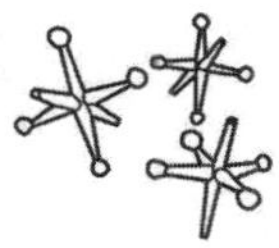

Ⓒ 

**4.** What does the word *rush* mean?

Ⓐ move quickly

Ⓑ move slowly

Ⓒ move quietly

**SCORE**

1. ☺ 😐

2. ☺ 😐

3. ☺ 😐

4. ☺ 😐

____ / 4
Total

NAME:________________________ DATE:________________

# At the Movies

Jon and Mark walk from the subway to a movie theater. First, they get in line to buy the tickets. Then they get some popcorn. They find two good seats inside. The movie lasts two hours. Jon and Mark laugh a lot. Soon it is time to go home again.

NAME: ______________________ DATE: ______________

**DIRECTIONS** Read "At the Movies." Answer the questions.

SCORE

1. ☺☹
2. ☺☹
3. ☺☹
4. ☺☹

___ / 4
Total

**1.** What kind of movie do you think it was?

- (A) It was about a war.
- (B) It was about something scary.
- (C) It was about something funny.

**2.** Where do Jon and Mark sit?

- (A) in line
- (B) by the popcorn
- (C) next to each other

**3.** What will Jon and Mark do next?

- (A) read a book
- (B) walk back to the subway
- (C) see one more movie

**4.** Which sentence best tells about this text?

- (A) Jon and Mark go to the movies.
- (B) Jon and Mark go to the subway.
- (C) Jon and Mark go home.

NAME: ____________________ DATE: ______________

SCORE

___ / 4

**Reread** "At the Movies."

**Think about** your favorite movie.

**Write about** the movie and why you like it.

**NAME:** ____________________ **DATE:** ______________

**DIRECTIONS** Read the text. Answer the questions.

A fox has sharp teeth. They are shaped to help it rip and tear. The small back teeth help it chew bones.

**1.** What word tells about fox teeth?

(A) flat

(B) sharp

(C) square

**2.** What does a fox do with its back teeth?

(A) chew bones

(B) chew trees

(C) chew grass

**3.** Which word does **not** have the same beginning sound as *sharp*?

(A) small

(B) share

(C) sugar

**4.** What is the opposite of *small*?

(A) front

(B) big

(C) tiny

**SCORE**

1. ☺ 😐

2. ☺ 😐

3. ☺ 😐

4. ☺ 😐

___ / 4
Total

**NAME:** ____________________ **DATE:** ______________

**DIRECTIONS** Read the text. Answer the questions.

SCORE

1. ☺ 😐
2. ☺ 😐
3. ☺ 😐
4. ☺ 😐

____ / 4
Total

Rabbit teeth never stop growing. They wear down when rabbits eat. Some teeth grow in crooked. They should be taken out!

**1.** Rabbit teeth are **not** like your teeth. How?

- (A) They wear down from eating.
- (B) They keep growing.
- (C) They eat carrots.

**2.** How do rabbit teeth wear down?

- (A) They just keep growing.
- (B) They grow in crooked.
- (C) They wear down when the rabbit eats.

**3.** The word *growing* has two parts: *grow* and *–ing.* Which word has two parts?

- (A) crooked
- (B) down
- (C) wear

**4.** What does the word *crooked* mean?

- (A) hard
- (B) straight
- (C) bent

 

**NAME:** ______________________ **DATE:** ______________

**DIRECTIONS** Read the text. Answer the questions.

Cows do not eat meat. They do not need sharp teeth to rip and tear. They eat grass. Most cow teeth are flat for chewing.

**1.** Why do cows **not** have sharp teeth?

- (A) They do not need to tear meat.
- (B) They chew bones and grass.
- (C) They wear them down by chewing meat.

**2.** What do cows eat?

- (A) bones
- (B) meat
- (C) grass

**3.** Which word has the same vowel sound as 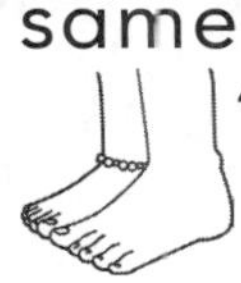 ?

- (A) are
- (B) tear
- (C) meat

**4.** Who does *they* refer to in this text?

- (A) teeth
- (B) cows
- (C) mean

**SCORE**

1. ☺ 😐

2. ☺ 😐

3. ☺ 😐

4. ☺ 😐

____ / 4

Total

**NAME:** ____________________ **DATE:** ____________

# Dinosaur Teeth

You can learn a lot by looking at dinosaur teeth. Some dinosaurs had teeth shaped like spoons. The diplodocus (dih-PLOD-uh-kuhs) scooped leaves from trees. But it did not chew the leaves. Its guts did all the work. Some dinosaurs had pointed teeth. Some had no teeth at all!

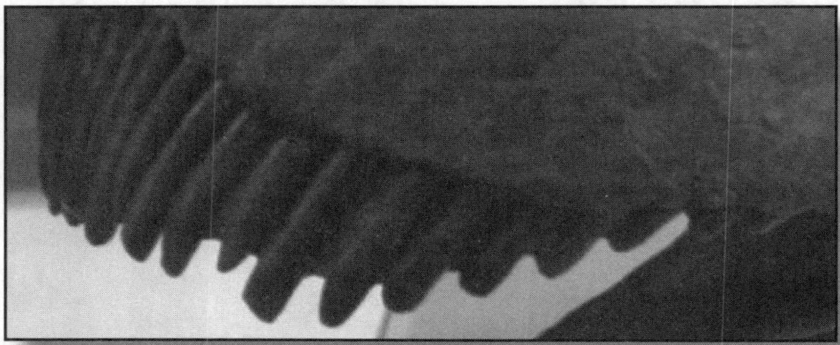

**diplodocus teeth**

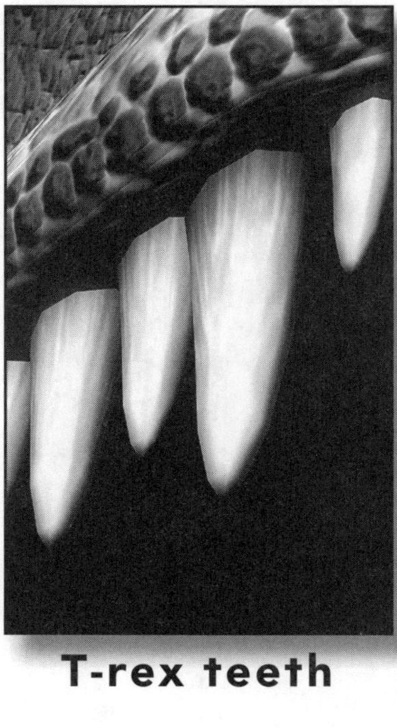

**T-rex teeth**

 

**NAME:** ______________________ **DATE:** ________________

**DIRECTIONS** Read "Dinosaur Teeth." Answer the questions.

**SCORE**

1. ☺ ☹
2. ☺ ☹
3. ☺ ☹
4. ☺ ☹

____ / 4
**Total**

**1.** Why would you want to look at dinosaur teeth?

Ⓐ to learn how to care for teeth
Ⓑ to learn about the animal
Ⓒ to learn about good food to eat

**2.** What is **not** a shape of dinosaur teeth?

Ⓐ round
Ⓑ pointed
Ⓒ spoon-shaped

**3.** What do you think dinosaurs without teeth ate?

Ⓐ soft food like fruit
Ⓑ meat and other dinosaurs
Ⓒ trees and bushes

**4.** What is the main idea?

Ⓐ Dinosaurs eat grass and leaves.
Ⓑ You should take good care of your teeth.
Ⓒ You can learn about dinosaurs from their teeth.

**NAME:** ______________________ **DATE:** ______________

SCORE

___ / 4

**Reread** "Dinosaur Teeth."

**Think about** when dinosaurs lived. What would you like to see if you could visit the time of dinosaurs?

**Write about** your visit and what you would eat.

 

**NAME:** ______________________ **DATE:** ______________

**DIRECTIONS** Read the text. Answer the questions.

Jin wants to make some money. Mom says, "I have two jobs you can do. You can rake the leaves. Then you can dig up the garden."

**1.** Who gives Jin a job?

Ⓐ the leaves
Ⓑ Mom
Ⓒ Dad

**2.** Why does Jin need a job?

Ⓐ Jin wants some money.
Ⓑ Jin likes to work.
Ⓒ Mom wants Jin to work.

**3.** The word *garden* has two syllables: *gar–den*. Which word has two syllables?

Ⓐ rake
Ⓑ leaves
Ⓒ money

**4.** What is another word for *then*?

Ⓐ next
Ⓑ last
Ⓒ first

**SCORE**

1. ☺ 😐
2. ☺ 😐
3. ☺ 😐
4. ☺ 😐

____ / 4 Total

**NAME:** ____________________ **DATE:** ______________

**DIRECTIONS** Read the text. Answer the questions.

SCORE

1. ☺ 😐

2. ☺ 😐

3. ☺ 😐

4. ☺ 😐

____ / 4
Total

Jin rakes and digs up the garden. She wants to work some more. Mom says, "You can take out the trash now."

**1.** Where does Jin work?

Ⓐ in the garden

Ⓑ in the house

Ⓒ at school

**2.** What jobs did Jin do?

Ⓐ She rakes and mows the yard.

Ⓑ She rakes and sweeps the leaves.

Ⓒ She rakes and digs up the garden.

**3.** Which word ends with the same sound as *trash*?

Ⓐ 

Ⓑ 

Ⓒ 

**4.** What does the word *trash* mean?

Ⓐ things to throw out

Ⓑ things to fix

Ⓒ things to put away

**NAME:** ______________________ **DATE:** ______________

**DIRECTIONS** Read the text. Answer the questions.

Mom tells Jin there is one big chore to do. "You need to clean your bedroom."

Jin asks, "Do I have to?"

**1.** Where does Jin have a chore to do?

(A) the kitchen
(B) the garden
(C) her bedroom

**2.** How does Jin feel about cleaning?

(A) Jin likes a clean bedroom.
(B) Jin does not like chores.
(C) Jin likes to help her mom.

**3.** Which word rhymes with ?

(A) there
(B) chore
(C) bedroom

**4.** What does the word *chore* mean?

(A) surprise
(B) game
(C) job

**SCORE**

1. ☺ 😐

2. ☺ 😐

3. ☺ 😐

4. ☺ 😐

___ / 4
Total

**NAME:** ______________________ **DATE:** ______________

# A Surprise Gift

Jin goes to the store. She looks at hats, mittens, and scarves. She buys a long, red scarf. She says to the clerk, "Would you please wrap this up?" Soon Jin is home. "Mom!" Jin says. "Where are you? I have a surprise for you!"

NAME: ____________________ DATE: ______________

**DIRECTIONS** Read "A Surprise Gift." Answer the questions.

**1.** Why did Jin ask to have the scarf wrapped?

(A) The scarf was a gift.

(B) The scarf was red.

(C) The scarf was pretty.

**2.** Who goes to the store with Jin?

(A) Jin goes with the clerk.

(B) Jin goes by herself.

(C) Jin goes with her mom.

**3.** What did Jin **not** look at?

(A) scarves

(B) a pair of mittens

(C) a pair of socks

**4.** Why do you think Jin got the gift?

(A) Jin did not want to work anymore.

(B) Her mom had a birthday.

(C) Jin had a birthday.

**SCORE**

1. ☺ 😐

2. ☺ 😐

3. ☺ 😐

4. ☺ 😐

____ / 4
Total

**NAME:** ____________________ **DATE:** ______________

SCORE

___/4

**Reread** "A Surprise Gift."

**Think about** a surprise you have had. Maybe you got a gift. Maybe you got to do something fun.

**Write about** your surprise.

 

**NAME:** ______________________ **DATE:** ______________

**DIRECTIONS** Read the text. Answer the questions.

SCORE

1. ☺ 😐

2. ☺ 😐

3. ☺ 😐

4. ☺ 😐

____ / 4 Total

It is hard to keep from getting a cold. You cannot see cold germs. Germs can live for days on things you may touch.

**1.** Why is it hard **not** to get a cold?

- (A) Germs die quickly.
- (B) Germs are easy to see.
- (C) Germs cannot be seen.

**2.** How might you get a cold germ?

- (A) by touching something with germs
- (B) by eating some foods
- (C) by touching something clean

**3.** Which picture shows a word that ends with the same two sounds as *germ*?

- (A) 
- (B) 
- (C) 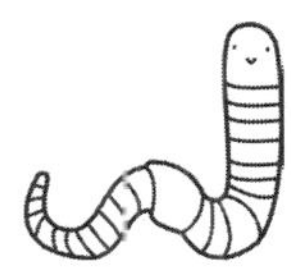

**4.** What does *getting a cold* mean?

- (A) becoming sick
- (B) feeling chilly
- (C) getting a coat

**NAME:** ____________________ **DATE:** ______________

**DIRECTIONS** Read the text. Answer the questions.

SCORE

1. ☺ 😐

2. ☺ 😐

3. ☺ 😐

4. ☺ 😐

____ / 4
Total

Most colds are passed by germs on hands. Wash your hands with soap and water. You can use special hand wipes that kill germs, too.

**1.** What is a good way to get rid of cold germs?

Ⓐ putting your hands in your pockets

Ⓑ washing your hands a lot

Ⓒ staying in the house a lot

**2.** How do you get most cold germs?

Ⓐ from germs on your hands

Ⓑ by getting wet and cold

Ⓒ from too much water

**3.** Which picture shows a word that has the same middle sound as *soap*?

Ⓐ 

Ⓑ 

Ⓒ 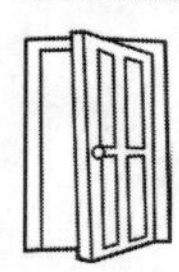

**4.** What does *special hand wipes* mean?

Ⓐ things made for cleaning your hands

Ⓑ cloths made for scrubbing things

Ⓒ things made for cleaning your face

 

**NAME:** ______________________ **DATE:** ______________

**DIRECTIONS** Read the text. Answer the questions.

Are you going to sneeze? Do not cover a sneeze with your hands. Use a tissue and toss it in the trash. Or sneeze into your elbow.

**1.** Why should you **not** sneeze into your hands?

Ⓐ Your hands can make you sicker.

Ⓑ You can pass the germs with your hands.

Ⓒ You can stop the germs with your hands.

**2.** What should you do if you do not have a tissue?

Ⓐ Sneeze into one hand.

Ⓑ Turn your head.

Ⓒ Sneeze into your elbow.

**3.** Which is the correct spelling for  ?

Ⓐ elbow

Ⓑ lbow

Ⓒ elbo

**4.** Where should you toss a tissue?

Ⓐ in the trash

Ⓑ on the ground

Ⓒ out the door

**SCORE**

1. ☺ 😐

2. ☺ 😐

3. ☺ 😐

4. ☺ 😐

____ / 4
Total

**NAME:** ____________________ **DATE:** ____________

# Fight Back!

You can help your body fight cold germs. Do not eat a lot of junk food. Eat good foods like fruit and vegetables. Do not have drinks with lots of sugar. Drink lots of water instead. Do not be a couch potato! Get out and take a walk.

**NAME:** ____________________ **DATE:** ______________

**DIRECTIONS** Read "Fight Back!" Answer the questions.

**SCORE**

1. ☺ ☹
2. ☺ ☹
3. ☺ ☹
4. ☺ ☹

___ / 4
Total

**1.** Why should you want to fight cold germs?

Ⓐ Getting a cold keeps you busy.

Ⓑ Getting a cold is better than the flu.

Ⓒ Getting a cold makes you feel bad.

**2.** Which would be good food choices to stay healthy?

Ⓐ chips and cookies

Ⓑ bananas and water

Ⓒ potatoes and fruit punch

**3.** Why should you take a walk?

Ⓐ It helps you stay strong.

Ⓑ It helps you catch a cold.

Ⓒ It helps you eat more food.

**4.** What is the main idea?

Ⓐ You should stay in bed if you get a cold.

Ⓑ You can help yourself fight colds.

Ⓒ You should see a doctor if you get a cold.

**NAME:** ______________________ **DATE:** ______________

SCORE

___ / 4

**Reread** "Fight Back!"

**Think about** all you have read about colds.

**Write about** things you can do that will help you fight a cold. Make a list.

 

**NAME:** ____________________ **DATE:** ______________

**DIRECTIONS** Read the text. Answer the questions.

**SCORE**

1. ☺ 😐

2. ☺ 😐

3. ☺ 😐

4. ☺ 😐

___ / 4
Total

Kim says, "Mom, can you help me find my turtle? He is missing. I have looked everywhere for him."

**1.** To whom is Kim talking?

- (A) her turtle
- (B) her dad
- (C) her mom

**2.** What is Kim's problem?

- (A) She needs to feed her turtle.
- (B) Her turtle is gone.
- (C) Mom needs to help Kim.

**3.** The word *missing* has two parts. What are the two parts?

- (A) *miss* and *–ing*
- (B) *mis* and *–ing*
- (C) *missi* and *–ng*

**4.** What is another word for *looked*?

- (A) glasses
- (B) gone
- (C) searched

**NAME:** ______________________________ **DATE:** ________________

**DIRECTIONS** Read the text. Answer the questions.

**SCORE**

1. ☺ ☹
2. ☺ ☹
3. ☺ ☹
4. ☺ ☹

___ / 4
Total

Mom says, "I think your turtle Tork is hiding."

"Why?" asks Kim.

"Winter is coming. Box turtles sleep a lot in winter," Mom says.

**1.** What is the name of the turtle?

Ⓐ Kim
Ⓑ Tork
Ⓒ Box

**2.** Why is the turtle hiding?

Ⓐ to find a place to sleep
Ⓑ to find food
Ⓒ to find a bed

**3.** The word *hiding* comes from *hide*. What word does *riding* come from?

Ⓐ rid
Ⓑ ride
Ⓒ ding

**4.** What is *a turtle*?

Ⓐ a brother
Ⓑ an animal
Ⓒ a hiding place

**NAME:** ____________________ **DATE:** ____________

**DIRECTIONS** Read the text. Answer the questions.

**SCORE**

1. ☺ 😐
2. ☺ 😐
3. ☺ 😐
4. ☺ 😐

____ / 4
Total

Kim says, "Why does Tork want to sleep?"

"Turtles slow down in winter," Mom says. "They sleep all winter, like bears. We should look for quiet and cool places."

**1.** Which animals slow down in winter?

- (A) turtles
- (B) frogs
- (C) dogs

**2.** Why would a turtle like a quiet place?

- (A) so it can eat alone
- (B) so it can sleep
- (C) so it can find water

**3.** Which word has the long *o* sound?

- (A) for
- (B) slow
- (C) cool

**4.** Who does *they* refer to in the text?

- (A) turtles
- (B) Kim and her mom
- (C) bears

**NAME:** ______________________ **DATE:** ______________

# Finding Tork

Kim and Mom find Tork in the closet.

Kim asks, "When will he wake up?"

Mom says, "Tork will wake up when he gets hungry."

Kim checks on Tork as he sleeps all winter. One day, he is not in the closet. Tork is right by his tank. He is ready to eat!

**NAME:** ______________________ **DATE:** ______________

**DIRECTIONS** Read "Finding Tork." Answer the questions.

**SCORE**

1. ☺ 😐
2. ☺ 😐
3. ☺ 😐
4. ☺ 😐

____ / 4
**Total**

**1.** Why does Kim check on Tork?

Ⓐ She wants to put him in his tank.

Ⓑ She wants to give him water.

Ⓒ She wants to be sure he is okay.

**2.** How do you think Kim feels when she finds Tork?

Ⓐ thankful

Ⓑ upset

Ⓒ tired

**3.** Why is Tork in the closet?

Ⓐ to eat

Ⓑ to get dressed

Ⓒ to sleep

**4.** What has Kim learned?

Ⓐ that turtles can sleep for months

Ⓑ that turtles like winter

Ⓒ that turtles like to be pets

NAME: ____________________ DATE: ____________

SCORE

___ / 4

**Reread** "Finding Tork."

**Think about** all the places turtles can sleep.

**Write about** a turtle that is looking for a place to sleep.

 

**NAME:** ______________________ **DATE:** ______________

**DIRECTIONS** Read the text. Answer the questions.

**SCORE**

1. ☺ 😐
2. ☺ 😐
3. ☺ 😐
4. ☺ 😐

___ / 4
Total

Black bears eat all summer long. They love fruit, nuts, and roots. They can gain 30 pounds in one week. That is a lot!

**1.** Which sentence is true?

- (A) Black bears get thinner in summer.
- (B) Black bears eat less in summer.
- (C) Black bears get fatter in summer.

**2.** What do black bears like to eat?

- (A) hay and grass
- (B) nuts and fruit
- (C) trees and bushes

**3.** The word summer has two syllables: *sum-mer*. Which word has two syllables?

- (A) better
- (B) asked
- (C) where

**4.** What is the opposite of *love*?

- (A) like
- (B) hate
- (C) friend

**NAME:** ____________________ **DATE:** ____________

**DIRECTIONS** Read the text. Answer the questions.

**SCORE**

1. ☺ 😐

2. ☺ 😐

3. ☺ 😐

4. ☺ 😐

___ / 4
**Total**

Black bears make a den in the fall. They may find a cave or a hole in a tree. They gather leaves and twigs for a nest.

**1.** What do black bears do in the fall?

Ⓐ find a place to eat

Ⓑ find a place for a den

Ⓒ find a place for food

**2.** What do bears use to make a den?

Ⓐ leaves and twigs

Ⓑ feathers

Ⓒ rocks and trees

**3.** Which word rhymes with *nest*?

Ⓐ 

Ⓑ 

Ⓒ 

**4.** What does the word *den* mean?

Ⓐ a place to eat

Ⓑ a place to wash

Ⓒ a place to live

**NAME:** ____________________ **DATE:** ____________

**DIRECTIONS** Read the text. Answer the questions.

SCORE

1. ☺ 😐
2. ☺ 😐
3. ☺ 😐
4. ☺ 😐

___ / 4
Total

The black bear goes into its den when winter starts. It curls up in a ball. Its head and paws stay warm while it sleeps.

**1.** What does the bear do when fall ends?

- (A) curls up in its den
- (B) eats food in its den
- (C) makes a warm nest

**2.** Why does the bear curl up?

- (A) to help it stay warm
- (B) to help it stay quiet
- (C) to help it eat

**3.** Which word has the same vowel sound as *start*?

- (A) 
- (B) 
- (C) 

**4.** Which other animals have paws?

- (A) horses
- (B) cows
- (C) dogs

**NAME:** ____________________ **DATE:** ____________

# A Very Long Nap

You may sleep for ten hours. The black bear can sleep for 100 days! Its body slows down while it hibernates. It lives on all the fat in its body. Bears wake up in the spring. They are much thinner. It is time for a big breakfast!

NAME: ______________________ DATE: ______________

**DIRECTIONS** Read "A Very Long Nap." Answer the questions.

**1.** Why is a bear thinner in spring?

Ⓐ It has used up its body fat.

Ⓑ It has been running a lot.

Ⓒ It has eaten fruit and roots.

**2.** What do bears do when they hibernate?

Ⓐ eat

Ⓑ sleep

Ⓒ talk

**3.** How are you like a black bear?

Ⓐ You both have paws.

Ⓑ You both sleep in a nest.

Ⓒ You both eat and sleep.

**4.** What is another good title for this text?

Ⓐ Hungry Bear

Ⓑ Asleep for Winter

Ⓒ Wake Up

**SCORE**

1. ☺ 😐

2. ☺ 😐

3. ☺ 😐

4. ☺ 😐

____ / 4
Total

**NAME:** ______________________ **DATE:** ______________

SCORE

___/4

**Reread** "A Very Long Nap."

**Think about** how bears spend winters sleeping.

**Write about** what you think a bear feels like when it wakes up in the spring.

 

**NAME:** ____________________ **DATE:** ______________

**DIRECTIONS** Read the text. Answer the questions.

**SCORE**

1. ☺ 😐

2. ☺ 😐

3. ☺ 😐

4. ☺ 😐

___ / 4
Total

Juan and Marie look out the window and see all white.

"No school today!" says Mom.

"Let's build a snowman!" Juan says.

"I'll get a carrot," Marie says. "Let's hurry!"

**1.** Why is there no school?

Ⓐ It is a Sunday.

Ⓑ It is summer.

Ⓒ It snowed a lot.

**2.** Why does Marie say she will get a carrot?

Ⓐ to eat as a snack

Ⓑ to make the snowman's nose

Ⓒ for Juan

**3.** The word *snowman* is made of two words: *snow* and *man*. Which picture shows a word made of two words?

Ⓐ 

Ⓑ 

Ⓒ 

**4.** What does the word *white* mean?

Ⓐ a food

Ⓑ a color

Ⓒ a toy

**NAME:** ____________________ **DATE:** ______________

**DIRECTIONS** Read the text. Answer the questions.

SCORE

1. ☺ 😐
2. ☺ 😐
3. ☺ 😐
4. ☺ 😐

___ / 4
Total

Juan and Marie roll a big ball of snow first. It will be the base. Juan rolls the middle ball next. Marie makes the head last.

**1.** Who rolls the last ball of snow?

- (A) Juan
- (B) Marie
- (C) Mom

**2.** Which ball is the base?

- (A) the biggest snowball
- (B) the middle snowball
- (C) the smallest snowball

**3.** Which is the correct spelling for  ?

- (A) hed
- (B) head
- (C) heed

**4.** What is the opposite of *last*?

- (A) the end
- (B) then
- (C) first

**NAME:** ______________________ **DATE:** ______________

**DIRECTIONS** Read the text. Answer the questions.

> The snowman gets big. Mom helps put the head on. Juan gets two branches for arms. "We are almost done!" says Marie.

**1.** Who gets the branches?

- (A) Mom
- (B) Juan
- (C) Marie

**2.** What are the branches for?

- (A) the arms
- (B) the feet
- (C) the smile

**3.** Which word rhymes with  ?

- (A) arms
- (B) done
- (C) snowman

**4.** What does *almost done* mean?

- (A) There is a little more to do.
- (B) There is a lot more to do.
- (C) There is no more to do.

**SCORE**

1.

2.

3.

4.

___ / 4
**Total**

NAME: ______________________ DATE: ______________

# Something Missing

Juan gives the snowman rocks for eyes and a smile. Marie wraps a scarf around its neck. She adds a carrot for the nose. Mom adds a hat and broom.

Then Mom says, "There is something missing."

"What?" Juan and Marie ask.

"A snow woman!" says Mom.

"You're right!" says Juan.

"Let's get to work!" says Marie.

**NAME:** ______________________ **DATE:** ______________

**DIRECTIONS** Read "Something Missing." Answer the questions.

**SCORE**

1. ☺ ☹

2. ☺ ☹

3. ☺ ☹

4. ☺ ☹

____ / 4

**Total**

**1.** Which might a snow woman wear?

Ⓐ 

Ⓑ 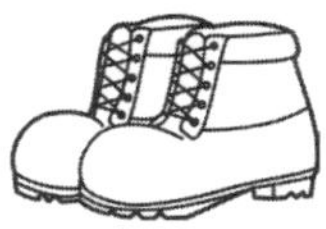

Ⓒ 

**2.** What is used to make the snowman's face?

Ⓐ buttons and a twig

Ⓑ a scarf and hat

Ⓒ rocks and a carrot

**3.** Why does Mom say that something is missing?

Ⓐ She thinks they should take a break.

Ⓑ She thinks they should make a snow woman.

Ⓒ She thinks they should get warm.

**4.** Which sentence best tells about this text?

Ⓐ It is fun to build snow people.

Ⓑ The family forgot to build a snowman.

Ⓒ It is too much work to build snow people.

**NAME:** ______________________ **DATE:** ______________

**SCORE**

___ /4

**Reread** "Something Missing."

**Think about** building a snowman. You can use almost anything to decorate them.

**Write about** what you would have a snowman wear.

**NAME:** ____________________ **DATE:** ______________

**DIRECTIONS** Read the text. Answer the questions.

SCORE

1. ☺ 😐

2. ☺ 😐

3. ☺ 😐

4. ☺ 😐

____ / 4
Total

A snowstorm can be fun. You can have a snowball fight. You can make a snowman. But a blizzard is not fun!

**1.** What can you do after it snows?

Ⓐ have a blizzard
Ⓑ play in the snow
Ⓒ stay inside

**2.** What is **not** fun?

Ⓐ a snowball fight
Ⓑ making a snowman
Ⓒ a blizzard

**3.** Which word has the same ending sound as *snow*?

Ⓐ go
Ⓑ bowl
Ⓒ hole

**4.** What is a *snowball fight*?

Ⓐ when you throw snowballs at each other
Ⓑ when you make blocks of snow
Ⓒ when you make a snowman

NAME:____________________ DATE:____________

**DIRECTIONS** Read the text. Answer the questions.

SCORE

1. ☺ ☹
2. ☺ ☹
3. ☺ ☹
4. ☺ ☹

____ / 4
Total

A snowstorm may not be a blizzard. The wind must be so strong that it is hard to see. It is very cold out, too. That is a blizzard.

**1.** Which sentence is true?

Ⓐ All storms have cold snow.

Ⓑ All snowstorms are blizzards.

Ⓒ A blizzard must have a strong wind.

**2.** Why is it hard to see in a blizzard?

Ⓐ There is a strong wind blowing the snow.

Ⓑ There is a lot of rain and hail.

Ⓒ It is dark when the snow falls.

**3.** Which word has the same vowel sound as *wind*?

Ⓐ out

Ⓑ blizzard

Ⓒ that

**4.** Which of these is also *very cold*?

Ⓐ a freezer

Ⓑ a bedroom

Ⓒ a chair

 

**NAME:** ____________________ **DATE:** ______________

**DIRECTIONS** Read the text. Answer the questions.

**SCORE**

1. ☺ ☹

2. ☺ ☹

3. ☺ ☹

4. ☺ ☹

___ / 4
Total

Some blizzards last for a long time. Snow piles up from the wind. Snowdrifts can even cover a car! Stay inside where it is safe.

**1.** What is this text about?

Ⓐ what happens in a blizzard

Ⓑ staying inside where it is safe

Ⓒ wind blowing hard

**2.** Why should you stay inside?

Ⓐ It can be unsafe outside during a blizzard.

Ⓑ You do not want to miss school.

Ⓒ You can wear warm clothes outside.

**3.** The word *inside* is made of two words: *in* and *side*. Which word is made of two words?

Ⓐ monkey

Ⓑ umbrella

Ⓒ backpack

**4.** What is another word for *piles*?

Ⓐ makes

Ⓑ stacks

Ⓒ plays

**NAME:** ______________________ **DATE:** ______________

# Get Ready and Stay Safe

Do you live in blizzard country? Get ready for winter. Keep snacks, water, and blankets in your car. Try to stay in the house during a blizzard. If you must go outside, cover up. The cold wind can hurt your skin. If you get very cold, you may get sleepy. Keep moving. Try to find a safe, warm place.

NAME: ____________________ DATE: ______________

**DIRECTIONS** Read "Get Ready and Stay Safe." Answer the questions.

SCORE

1. ☺ 😐
2. ☺ 😐
3. ☺ 😐
4. ☺ 😐

____ / 4
Total

**1.** Why should you cover up if you go outside in a blizzard?

Ⓐ to keep awake when you walk

Ⓑ to keep rested and have fun

Ⓒ to keep your body warm and safe

**2.** How can you get ready for a blizzard?

Ⓐ Keep extra food and water in your car.

Ⓑ Take long walks in the snow.

Ⓒ Eat a big lunch and take a nap.

**3.** When do blizzards often happen?

Ⓐ in summer

Ⓑ in winter

Ⓒ all year

**4.** What is the main idea?

Ⓐ Know what kind of day it will be.

Ⓑ Know what to keep in your car.

Ⓒ Know how to stay safe in a blizzard.

NAME: ____________________ DATE: ______________

SCORE

___ / 4

**Reread** "Get Ready and Stay Safe."

**Think about** the times you have been in a storm. It could be a blizzard or a rainstorm. It could be a sandstorm. It could be a tornado. What did you do to stay safe?

**Write about** ways to stay safe in any storm.

 

**NAME:** ____________________ **DATE:** ______________

**DIRECTIONS** Read the text. Answer the questions.

SCORE

1. ☺ 😐
2. ☺ 😐
3. ☺ 😐
4. ☺ 😐

____ / 4
Total

Miss Parker talks with her class. "We are going to have an art show! We have three weeks to get ready," she says.

**1.** Who is Miss Parker?

Ⓐ a music teacher

Ⓑ an art teacher

Ⓒ a nurse

**2.** What does the class need to get ready for?

Ⓐ making art

Ⓑ their class

Ⓒ the art show

**3.** Which word ends with the same sound as  ?

Ⓐ show

Ⓑ to

Ⓒ going

**4.** What does it mean to *get ready*?

Ⓐ to get the show set up

Ⓑ to get the show over with

Ⓒ to clean up after the show

**NAME:** ______________________ **DATE:** ______________

**DIRECTIONS** Read the text. Answer the questions.

SCORE

1. ☺ 😐

2. ☺ 😐

3. ☺ 😐

4. ☺ 😐

___ / 4
Total

"Class, please decide what to make for the art show. You can use clay, paper, or paint. You may also think of something new," says Miss Parker.

**1.** Who is talking?

Ⓐ a parent

Ⓑ the teacher

Ⓒ the children

**2.** What can the children do?

Ⓐ make something with clay, paint, or paper

Ⓑ make music for a new song

Ⓒ read a book about making art

**3.** The word *something* is made of two words: *some* and *thing.* Which word is also made of two words?

Ⓐ shovel

Ⓑ shadow

Ⓒ shoelaces

**4.** What is *paint*?

Ⓐ a toy

Ⓑ an art supply

Ⓒ a food

 

**NAME:** ____________________ **DATE:** ______________

**DIRECTIONS** Read the text. Answer the questions.

**SCORE**

1. ☺ 😐

2. ☺ 😐

3. ☺ 😐

4. ☺ 😐

___ / 4 Total

Jen, Ted, and Chris decide to work as a team. They each make some fish out of clay. They let the fish dry. Then, they paint them.

**1.** Who makes a team?

- (A) Jen, Ted, and Chris
- (B) the clay fish
- (C) the paint

**2.** What do they do last?

- (A) color
- (B) paint
- (C) draw

**3.** Which word ends with the same sound as  ?

- (A) clay
- (B) dry
- (C) Jen

**4.** Who does *them* refer to in this text?

- (A) Jen and Chris
- (B) the team
- (C) the clay fish

**NAME:** ______________________ **DATE:** ______________

# The Best Fish

The day of the class art show comes. Chris, Jen, and Ted have put their clay fish into a fishbowl. Chris and Jen add rocks and shells. Ted puts in a small plant. It looks as if their fish were in the sea. All of the art pieces look great. All of the children get a ribbon. But Chris, Jen, and Ted think their ribbon is best!

**NAME:** ____________________ **DATE:** ______________

**DIRECTIONS** Read "The Best Fish." Answer the questions.

**SCORE**

1. ☺ ☹
2. ☺ ☹
3. ☺ ☹
4. ☺ ☹

____ / 4
Total

**1.** Chris, Jen, and Ted think their ribbon is best. Why?

Ⓐ They are proud of their art.

Ⓑ They want a new ribbon.

Ⓒ They want to share a ribbon.

**2.** Where is the art show?

Ⓐ in a house

Ⓑ in a classroom

Ⓒ in a park

**3.** Why do they add more to the fishbowl?

Ⓐ to make it look like the sea

Ⓑ to make it look more fun

Ⓒ to make it have more color

**4.** What do you think they learned?

Ⓐ They like painting best.

Ⓑ They like working as a team.

Ⓒ They like having a fishbowl.

**NAME:** ______________________ **DATE:** ______________

SCORE

___/4

**Reread** "The Best Fish."

**Think about** what you would make for an art show. Think about what you would do first, second, and last.

**Write about** your art piece.

**NAME:** ______________________ **DATE:** ______________

**DIRECTIONS** Read the text. Answer the questions.

SCORE

1. ☺ ☹

2. ☺ ☹

3. ☺ ☹

4. ☺ ☹

___ / 4
Total

One winter day, Sherman Poppen saw his daughter stand on her sled. She rode it down the hill. It looked like a lot of fun to him.

**1.** What did Sherman Poppen see?

Ⓐ his daughter lying flat while riding her sled

Ⓑ his daughter sitting while riding her sled

Ⓒ his daughter standing while riding her sled

**2.** What did Sherman Poppen think about his daughter on her sled?

Ⓐ that she could fall off

Ⓑ that it must be fun

Ⓒ that she should sit down

**3.** Which picture shows a word that sounds just like *rode*?

Ⓐ 

Ⓑ 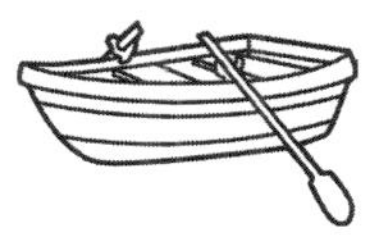

Ⓒ 

**4.** What is *winter*?

Ⓐ a color

Ⓑ a season

Ⓒ a food

**NAME:** ______________________ **DATE:** ______________

**DIRECTIONS** Read the text. Answer the questions.

SCORE

1. ☺ 😐
2. ☺ 😐
3. ☺ 😐
4. ☺ 😐

___ / 4 Total

Mr. Poppen had an idea. He got two skis. He tied them together. The skis made a board. His daughter stood on it and rode it down the hill.

**1.** What did Mr. Poppen use for his idea?

Ⓐ a sled
Ⓑ his workshop
Ⓒ two skis

**2.** What did he make?

Ⓐ something to sit on
Ⓑ something to stand on
Ⓒ something to lie on

**3.** The word *together* has three syllables: *to-geth-er*. Which word also has three syllables?

Ⓐ something
Ⓑ another
Ⓒ birthday

**4.** What does the word *idea* mean?

Ⓐ thought
Ⓑ talk
Ⓒ trick

 

**NAME:** ______________________ **DATE:** ______________

**DIRECTIONS** Read the text. Answer the questions.

**SCORE**

1. ☺ 😐
2. ☺ 😐
3. ☺ 😐
4. ☺ 😐

___ / 4
Total

Mr. Poppen added a rope to the front of the skis. Now it could be controlled. It was even more fun to ride. Now all the children wanted one!

**1.** How did Mr. Poppen make the skis better?

- Ⓐ He added a rope to the front.
- Ⓑ He added a rope to the back.
- Ⓒ He added a handle.

**2.** Why did all the children want one?

- Ⓐ There was snow outside.
- Ⓑ It looked like fun to ride.
- Ⓒ His daughter liked to share.

**3.** Which word rhymes with *could*?

- Ⓐ good
- Ⓑ gold
- Ⓒ pulled

**4.** What does *added* mean?

- Ⓐ to use
- Ⓑ to make
- Ⓒ to put something on

NAME: ______________________ DATE: ______________

# The Snurfer

Sherman Poppen had made a great toy. It needed a name. His wife called it a *snurfer*. Soon a toy company started making them. Lots of children used them for a few years. Later, people thought of ways to make them better. You may have used what came next: the snowboard!

**NAME:** ______________________ **DATE:** ______________

**DIRECTIONS** Read "The Snurfer." Answer the questions.

**SCORE**

1. ☺😐
2. ☺😐
3. ☺😐
4. ☺😐

____ / 4
Total

**1.** Which words do you think the word *snurfer* came from?

Ⓐ snow and surfer
Ⓑ sled and skis
Ⓒ sled and surf

**2.** How do you think a person steers a snurfer?

Ⓐ with a steering wheel
Ⓑ with a rope
Ⓒ with the rider's feet

**3.** Why did people make changes to the snurfer?

Ⓐ so it would work even better
Ⓑ so it would be even smaller
Ⓒ so it could be painted

**4.** What is the main idea?

Ⓐ The snowboard began with a toy called a snurfer.
Ⓑ Mrs. Poppen named a toy a snurfer.
Ⓒ A toy company made snurfers.

**NAME:** ______________________ **DATE:** ______________

SCORE

___ / 4

**Reread** "The Snurfer."

**Think about** the kinds of things you like to do outside. Maybe you use a skateboard. Maybe you like to ride a pogo stick. What could you do to make something you play with better?

**Write about** what you would like to make.

 

**NAME:** ______________________ **DATE:** ______________

**DIRECTIONS** Read the text. Answer the questions.

Zoe and Taj get ready for a trip. They pack sweaters and warm pants. They put on jackets, hats, scarves, and gloves.

**1.** Who is getting ready for a trip?

Ⓐ sweaters and pants
Ⓑ Zoe and Taj
Ⓒ jackets and hats

**2.** Which sentence is true?

Ⓐ They are going somewhere cold.
Ⓑ They are going somewhere hot.
Ⓒ They are going to a beach.

**3.** Which word is spelled correctly?

Ⓐ rede
Ⓑ reade
Ⓒ ready

**4.** *Scarves* means more than one what?

Ⓐ scar
Ⓑ scarve
Ⓒ scarf

**SCORE**

1. ☺ 😐
2. ☺ 😐
3. ☺ 😐
4. ☺ 😐

____ / 4
**Total**

 

**NAME:** ____________________ **DATE:** ____________

**DIRECTIONS** Read the text. Answer the questions.

SCORE

1. ☺ 😐

2. ☺ 😐

3. ☺ 😐

4. ☺ 😐

___ / 4
Total

Zoe and Taj are ready for a long drive in the car. It snows hard in the mountains. Dad stops to get hot chocolate.

**1.** Where are they driving?

Ⓐ to the city

Ⓑ to the mountains

Ⓒ to the forest

**2.** Why do you think they will have a long drive?

Ⓐ They are going a long way.

Ⓑ They are going to sleep in the car.

Ⓒ They are going home soon.

**3.** Which word has the same middle sound as *hard*?

Ⓐ Taj

Ⓑ bear

Ⓒ heart

**4.** What does *hard* mean in this text?

Ⓐ firm

Ⓑ a lot

Ⓒ soft

 

**NAME:** ______________________ **DATE:** ______________

**DIRECTIONS** Read the text. Answer the questions.

SCORE

1. ☺ 😐
2. ☺ 😐
3. ☺ 😐
4. ☺ 😐

____ / 4
Total

The family gets to their hotel long after dark. The next morning, Zoe and Taj put on their ski clothes. "Time for school!" Zoe says.

**1.** When does the family get to their hotel?

(A) late at night
(B) before dinner
(C) the next morning

**2.** Zoe says that it is time for school. What does she mean?

(A) They are going to do their homework.
(B) They are going to learn how to ski.
(C) They are going to learn how to ice skate.

**3.** The word *hotel* has two syllables: *ho-tel*. Which word also has two syllables?

(A) dark
(B) morning
(C) school

**4.** What is the opposite of *dark*?

(A) back
(B) dim
(C) light

**NAME:** ______________________________ **DATE:** ________________

## Ski School

Zoe and Taj take skiing lessons the first day. First, they learn how to get up after a fall. They fall down a lot. But it is still fun. That afternoon, they ride the ski lift to the top of a small hill. Soon they can zip down the hill without falling. They are skiers!

**NAME:** ____________________ **DATE:** ______________

**DIRECTIONS** Read "Ski School." Answer the questions.

**SCORE**

1. ☺ 😐
2. ☺ 😐
3. ☺ 😐
4. ☺ 😐

___ / 4 Total

**1.** What do you think they want to do the next day?

Ⓐ quit skiing
Ⓑ ride back home
Ⓒ go skiing again

**2.** What is a *ski lift*?

Ⓐ a chair that takes skiers up a hill
Ⓑ an elevator to help you lift skis
Ⓒ a pair of skis and poles

**3.** What other things might they do on this trip?

Ⓐ learn to use a skateboard
Ⓑ learn to water ski
Ⓒ learn to use a snowboard

**4.** Which is another good title for this text?

Ⓐ Learning to Ski
Ⓑ Learning the Mountain
Ⓒ Learning to Play

**NAME:** ______________________ **DATE:** ______________

SCORE

___ / 4

**Reread** "Ski School."

**Think about** what your best winter trip would be like. Would you like to learn to ice skate? Would you like to learn to use snowshoes?

**Write about** what you would like to do and why.

 

**NAME:** ______________________ **DATE:** ______________

**DIRECTIONS** Read the text. Answer the questions.

George Crum lived in the 1800s. He was a good chef. He often made a potato dish. He would slice potatoes and fry them.

**1.** What did Mr. Crum do?

- (A) cook potatoes
- (B) grow potatoes
- (C) sell potatoes

**2.** What is something Mr. Crum did **not** do to the potatoes?

- (A) slice them
- (B) bake them
- (C) fry them

**3.** The word *potato* has three syllables: *po-ta-to.* Which word also has three syllables?

- (A) surprise
- (B) window
- (C) kangaroo

**4.** What does a *chef* do?

- (A) clean up
- (B) cook food
- (C) serve food

**SCORE**

1. ☺ 😐

2. ☺ 😐

3. ☺ 😐

4. ☺ 😐

____ / 4 Total

**NAME:** ______________________ **DATE:** ______________

**DIRECTIONS** Read the text. Answer the questions.

**SCORE**

1. ☺ 😐

2. ☺ 😐

3. ☺ 😐

4. ☺ 😐

____ / 4
**Total**

One diner asked to have the fried potatoes. Mr. Crum fixed them for him. But the man did not like them. He said the potato slices were too thick.

**1.** What did the man want to eat?

Ⓐ potato salad

Ⓑ fried potatoes

Ⓒ a baked potato

**2.** The man did not like the potatoes. Why?

Ⓐ He wanted the potatoes to be thin.

Ⓑ He was not that hungry.

Ⓒ He did not want them fried.

**3.** Which word ends with the same sound as  ?

Ⓐ potato

Ⓑ diner

Ⓒ fried

**4.** What does the word *thick* mean?

Ⓐ wide

Ⓑ narrow

Ⓒ just right

**NAME:** ______________________ **DATE:** ________________

**DIRECTIONS** Read the text. Answer the questions.

**SCORE**

1. ☺ 😐
2. ☺ 😐
3. ☺ 😐
4. ☺ 😐

____ / 4
**Total**

Mr. Crum thought he would teach the man a lesson. So he sliced the potatoes very thin. He fried them until they were crisp.

**1.** How did Mr. Crum teach the man a lesson?

Ⓐ He made the potatoes very different.

Ⓑ He made the potatoes the same way.

Ⓒ He did not make potatoes at all.

**2.** What did Mr. Crum do to the potatoes?

Ⓐ He made them cold and hard.

Ⓑ He made them thin and crisp.

Ⓒ He made them thick and crisp.

**3.** The root word of *fried* is *fry*. What is the root word for *cried*?

Ⓐ crying

Ⓑ cry

Ⓒ crier

**4.** What is the opposite of *crisp*?

Ⓐ crunchy and hot

Ⓑ hard and dry

Ⓒ soft and mushy

**NAME:** ______________________ **DATE:** ______________

# A Basket of Crisps

George Crum got a big surprise. The diner liked the "crisps." He asked for more. Then other diners asked for them. A few years later, Mr. Crum had his own restaurant. All diners got crisps in a basket. You may have had these crisps, too. You know them as potato chips!

NAME:________________________ DATE:________________

**DIRECTIONS** Read "A Basket of Crisps." Answer the questions.

**1.** Why do you think the potatoes were first called *crisps*?

Ⓐ They were hard and thick.

Ⓑ They were soft and thin.

Ⓒ They were thin and crunchy.

**2.** How did Mr. Crum serve the crisps?

Ⓐ on a plate

Ⓑ in a basket

Ⓒ in a bag

**3.** Why was Mr. Crum surprised?

Ⓐ He did not like the crisps.

Ⓑ He did not think the diner would like the crisps.

Ⓒ He did not want to make the crisps.

**4.** What is another good title for this text?

Ⓐ The Beginning of Potato Chips

Ⓑ A Surprise Restaurant

Ⓒ The Life of a Chef

**SCORE**

1. ☺ 😐

2. ☺ 😐

3. ☺ 😐

4. ☺ 😐

____ / 4
Total

**NAME:** ______________________ **DATE:** ______________

SCORE

___ / 4

**Reread** "A Basket of Crisps."

**Think about** what Mr. Crum put on his tables. What do you like to eat at a restaurant? What would you put on the tables? Popcorn? Potato chips? Peanuts? Something else?

**Write about** what you would serve at a restaurant and why.

 

**NAME:** ______________________ **DATE:** ______________

**DIRECTIONS** Read the text. Answer the questions.

**SCORE**

1. ☺ 😐
2. ☺ 😐
3. ☺ 😐
4. ☺ 😐

____ / 4 Total

Matt and Sue like to play marbles. First, they put their marbles in the ring. Then they take turns trying to knock out the marbles.

**1.** Who is playing the game?

- (A) Matt and Sue
- (B) marbles
- (C) the ring

**2.** What do they try to do in the game?

- (A) They try to keep the marbles in the ring.
- (B) They try to knock the marbles out of the ring.
- (C) They try to make a bigger ring of marbles.

**3.** The word *marble* is made of two syllables: *mar-ble*. Which word is also made of two syllables?

- (A) animal
- (B) monkey
- (C) truck

**4.** What does *ring* mean in this text?

- (A) a circle
- (B) jewelry
- (C) group

NAME:______________________________ DATE:____________________

**DIRECTIONS** Read the text. Answer the questions.

SCORE

1. ☺ 😐
2. ☺ 😐
3. ☺ 😐
4. ☺ 😐

____ / 4
Total

Pete and Jenna like jacks. Ten jacks go on the floor. Pete tosses the ball up. It can bounce just one time. Pete picks up one jack and catches the ball.

**1.** Who plays jacks first?

Ⓐ Jenna
Ⓑ Pete
Ⓒ a ball and 10 jacks

**2.** What do you think happens if the ball bounces twice?

Ⓐ Pete stops the game.
Ⓑ Pete tries to pick up two jacks.
Ⓒ Pete loses his turn.

**3.** Which word rhymes with *floor*?

Ⓐ door
Ⓑ flour
Ⓒ were

**4.** What is the opposite of *up*?

Ⓐ out
Ⓑ in
Ⓒ down

**NAME:** ____________________ **DATE:** ______________

**DIRECTIONS** Read the text. Answer the questions.

SCORE

1. ☺ ☹

2. ☺ ☹

3. ☺ ☹

4. ☺ ☹

___ / 4
Total

All the children like to play shadow tag. One child is "It." But they don't touch each other. Instead, "It" tries to step on another's shadow. That child is now out.

**1.** What kind of weather is needed to play shadow tag?

Ⓐ cloudy weather

Ⓑ sunny weather

Ⓒ rainy weather

**2.** What does "It" try to do?

Ⓐ run faster

Ⓑ step on a shadow

Ⓒ keep away from a shadow

**3.** Which word has the same vowel sound as *touch*?

Ⓐ 

Ⓑ 

Ⓒ 

**4.** What does the word *out* mean in this text?

Ⓐ not in the house

Ⓑ not in the yard

Ⓒ not in the game

**NAME:** ______________________ **DATE:** ______________

# Tag in the Dark

Dad likes to play flashlight tag when it is dark. He is always "It" first. Dad uses a tree as the base. He counts to ten while the kids hide. Then Dad turns on the flashlight. He begins to look for the kids. They try to get back to the base. Soon Dad yells, "Pete!" Pete is caught in the light!

**NAME:** ______________________ **DATE:** ______________

**DIRECTIONS** Read "Tag in the Dark." Answer the questions.

**SCORE**

1. ☺ 😐
2. ☺ 😐
3. ☺ 😐
4. ☺ 😐

____ / 4
Total

**1.** Why does Dad count to ten?

- Ⓐ to give the children time to hide
- Ⓑ to give the children time to get flashlights
- Ⓒ to give the children time to run to the base

**2.** Why do they play flashlight tag in the dark?

- Ⓐ so they can play with flashlights
- Ⓑ so they can find their way to the base
- Ⓒ so Dad can catch them

**3.** What do you think will happen next?

- Ⓐ Pete is out of the game and goes home.
- Ⓑ Pete gets to be "It."
- Ⓒ Dad chooses Jenna to be "It."

**4.** What is the goal of the game?

- Ⓐ to get back to the base safely
- Ⓑ to learn to use a flashlight
- Ⓒ to get caught by Dad

**NAME:** ____________________ **DATE:** ____________

**SCORE**

___ / 4

**Reread** "Tag in the Dark."

**Think about** playing games. Which one do you like best?

**Write about** a good time you had playing a game with friends.

 

NAME: ____________________ DATE: ______________

**DIRECTIONS** Read the text. Answer the questions.

SCORE

1. ☺ ☹

2. ☺ ☹

3. ☺ ☹

4. ☺ ☹

___ / 4
Total

Some toys do not change much. Children have played with toy bears for more than 100 years. The early bears were called *teddy bears*.

**1.** Which is true?

Ⓐ Toy bears are a new kind of toy.

Ⓑ Kids have played with toy bears for a long time.

Ⓒ Kids do not play with toy bears much.

**2.** What were early bears called?

Ⓐ toy bears

Ⓑ baby bears

Ⓒ teddy bears

**3.** Which word begins with the same sound as *years*?

Ⓐ yes

Ⓑ bears

Ⓒ will

**4.** Which is **not** a toy?

Ⓐ teddy bear

Ⓑ cup

Ⓒ ball

**NAME:** ______________________ **DATE:** ______________

**DIRECTIONS** Read the text. Answer the questions.

SCORE

1. ☺ 😐

2. ☺ 😐

3. ☺ 😐

4. ☺ 😐

___ / 4
Total

One kind of old toy that children still like is Tinker Toys. The two men who made it liked strong toys. Tinker Toys are made of wood.

**1.** Who made Tinker Toys?

Ⓐ children

Ⓑ two men

Ⓒ wood

**2.** Why did the men use wood?

Ⓐ to make the toy fun

Ⓑ to make the toy strong

Ⓒ to make the toy big

**3.** Which word rhymes with *wood*?

Ⓐ good

Ⓑ food

Ⓒ wait

**4.** What is the opposite of *strong*?

Ⓐ weak

Ⓑ out

Ⓒ light

 

**NAME:** ____________________ **DATE:** ______________

**DIRECTIONS** Read the text. Answer the questions.

**SCORE**

1. ☺ 😐

2. ☺ 😐

3. ☺ 😐

4. ☺ 😐

___ / 4
**Total**

Do you have one dollar? Long ago, you could buy a windup toy for a dollar. Wind it up. Watch the frog hop, hop, hop!

**1.** Which sentence is true?

(A) Long ago, you could buy a frog for a dollar.
(B) Long ago, you could buy a toy for a dollar.
(C) Long ago, you would hop.

**2.** What kind of toy is it?

(A) a baby toy
(B) a windup toy
(C) a new toy

**3.** Which word is spelled correctly?

(A) dollr
(B) doler
(C) dollar

**4.** What does the word *wind* mean in this text?

(A) turn
(B) play
(C) blow

**NAME:**______________________________ **DATE:**________________

# Trains for All Ages

The first model trains were made more than 100 years ago. They showed what it was like to ride on a train. Then, toy makers found out that children of all ages love trains. They began to make model trains that cost less. Now, lots of people can have a simple train set. They can also build a full railway!

**NAME:** ____________________ **DATE:** ____________

**DIRECTIONS** Read "Trains for All Ages." Answer the questions.

**1.** What does *model* mean in this text?

- (A) an older kind of train
- (B) a small copy of a train
- (C) a track for a train

**2.** Which kind of train set would be simple?

- (A) a plain train set with one track
- (B) a full railway with three tracks
- (C) a set of two trains with a station

**3.** Why did toy makers make trains?

- (A) because people wanted to have their own toy train
- (B) because people wanted to go on train trips
- (C) because people could not go on train trips

**4.** What is another good title for this text?

- (A) Why We Take Train Trips
- (B) Why Toy Trains Cost Too Much
- (C) Why We Have Model Trains

**SCORE**

1. ☺ 😐

2. ☺ 😐

3. ☺ 😐

4. ☺ 😐

____ / 4 Total

**NAME:** ______________________ **DATE:** ______________

SCORE
___ / 4

**Reread** "Trains for All Ages."

**Think about** the trains you have seen. What would you like in a train set?

**Write about** what your train set would look like.

 

**NAME:** ______________________ **DATE:** ________________

**DIRECTIONS** Read the text. Answer the questions.

The Main Street School is having a winter fair. Kile and Dave get to the school gym early. They are excited. Maybe they will win some prizes!

**1.** Where is the fair being held?

Ⓐ at the Main Street School library

Ⓑ on the Main Street School playground

Ⓒ at the Main Street School gym

**2.** Why do you think Kile and Dave go early?

Ⓐ They can't wait to see the fair.

Ⓑ They woke up late that day.

Ⓒ They do not want to see much.

**3.** Which word rhymes with ?

Ⓐ excited

Ⓑ prize

Ⓒ winter

**4.** What does the word *fair* mean in this text?

Ⓐ share equally

Ⓑ magic show

Ⓒ carnival

**SCORE**

1. ☺ 😐

2. ☺ 😐

3. ☺ 😐

4. ☺ 😐

____ / 4
**Total**

NAME: ______________________ DATE: ______________

**DIRECTIONS** Read the text. Answer the questions.

SCORE

1. ☺ 😐

2. ☺ 😐

3. ☺ 😐

4. ☺ 😐

____ / 4
Total

Kile and Dave do the beanbag toss first. They each try to get three beanbags through the mouth of a wooden lion. They each miss once.

**1.** What game do they play first?

Ⓐ the baseball toss

Ⓑ the pillow toss

Ⓒ the beanbag toss

**2.** How many times does each get the beanbag through?

Ⓐ once

Ⓑ twice

Ⓒ three times

**3.** Which word begins with the same sound as *each*?

Ⓐ eel

Ⓑ eight

Ⓒ elf

**4.** Which word means the number 3?

Ⓐ tree

Ⓑ three

Ⓒ tee

 

**NAME:** ______________________ **DATE:** ______________

**DIRECTIONS** Read the text. Answer the questions.

**SCORE**

1. ☺ 😐

2. ☺ 😐

3. ☺ 😐

4. ☺ 😐

___ / 4
Total

Every child wins in the balloon-stomp game. There is a slip of paper in each balloon. The papers tell Kile and Dave what they have won.

**1.** Who plays the balloon-stomp game?

- (A) no one
- (B) a slip of paper
- (C) Kile and Dave

**2.** What is on each slip of paper?

- (A) the name of a prize
- (B) the name of a player
- (C) the color of the balloon

**3.** Which word sounds just like the word *won*?

- (A) one
- (B) own
- (C) on

**4.** What does the word *slip* mean in this text?

- (A) a piece of clothing
- (B) a small piece of something
- (C) to fall down

**NAME:** ______________________ **DATE:** ______________

# The Cakewalk

Kile and Dave do the cakewalk at the fair. They each stand on a square with a number on it. The music starts, and they walk in a circle. The music stops, and everyone stands on a square. The leader draws two numbers from a hat. Kile and Dave cheer. They each walk home with a big cake!

NAME: ______________________ DATE: ______________

**DIRECTIONS** Read "The Cakewalk." Answer the questions.

**1.** Why do you think Kile and Dave did the cakewalk?

Ⓐ They like to play a game.

Ⓑ They want to win a cake.

Ⓒ They are best friends.

**2.** What does the leader do?

Ⓐ She chooses the cakes from a table.

Ⓑ She chooses the winning numbers from a hat.

Ⓒ She chooses the winning names from a hat.

**3.** Why do Kile and Dave cheer?

Ⓐ They are ready to go home.

Ⓑ Their friends won cakes.

Ⓒ They each won a cake.

**4.** Which sentence best tells about this text?

Ⓐ Kile and Dave have fun.

Ⓑ Kile and Dave do the cakewalk.

Ⓒ Kile and Dave go home.

**SCORE**

1. ☺ 😐

2. ☺ 😐

3. ☺ 😐

4. ☺ 😐

___ / 4
Total

**NAME:** ______________________ **DATE:** ______________

SCORE

___ / 4

**Reread** "The Cakewalk."

**Think about** the different kinds of cake. Which one do you like the best?

**Write about** how your favorite cake looks and tastes.

**NAME:** ____________________ **DATE:** ______________

**DIRECTIONS** Read the text. Answer the questions.

SCORE

1. ☺ ☹
2. ☺ ☹
3. ☺ ☹
4. ☺ ☹

____ / 4 Total

James worked at a school for boys. He was in charge of sports. He needed an inside sport for children to play during cold winters.

**1.** What did James do for his job?

Ⓐ teach sports
Ⓑ teach art
Ⓒ teach math

**2.** Why did he need an inside sport?

Ⓐ It was more fun to play inside.
Ⓑ It was too hot to play outside.
Ⓒ It was too cold to play outside.

**3.** Which word starts with the same sound as *sports*?

Ⓐ pump
Ⓑ spider
Ⓒ inside

**4.** Which is **not** a sport?

Ⓐ baseball
Ⓑ reading
Ⓒ soccer

**NAME:** ______________________ **DATE:** ______________

**DIRECTIONS** Read the text. Answer the questions.

SCORE

1. ☺ 😐

2. ☺ 😐

3. ☺ 😐

4. ☺ 😐

___ / 4
Total

James wanted a game that could be played in a small space. He got a soccer ball. He got two peach baskets. Then he wrote down some rules.

**1.** What does James do?

(A) play soccer until lunchtime

(B) gather supplies to make a game

(C) pick peaches for presents

**2.** What does James get for the game?

(A) two peach baskets and two soccer balls

(B) two peach baskets and one soccer ball

(C) two peach baskets and a set of rules

**3.** The word *soccer* has two syllables: *soc-cer.* Which word has two syllables?

(A) but

(B) butterfly

(C) butter

**4.** Which is the word for the number 2?

(A) to

(B) two

(C) too

NAME: ______________________ DATE: ______________

**DIRECTIONS** Read the text. Answer the questions.

SCORE

1. ☺ 😐
2. ☺ 😐
3. ☺ 😐
4. ☺ 😐

____ / 4
Total

James tied each basket high on a railing. Each team tried to get the ball into the basket. But there was a big problem!

**1.** What did each team want to do?

- (A) run fast to a basket
- (B) get the ball in the basket
- (C) hit the basket with the ball

**2.** What do you think the problem is?

- (A) The basket was not high enough.
- (B) They only had one ball to throw.
- (C) The ball had to be taken out of the basket.

**3.** Which word sounds the same as *there*?

- (A) them
- (B) their
- (C) they

**4.** What does *problem* mean in this text?

- (A) something to be worked out
- (B) 2 + 2 = 4
- (C) finding out how deep the baskets are

**NAME:** ______________________ **DATE:** ______________

# A New Game

James called his game *basketball*. At first, players had to toss the ball back and forth to get to the baskets. Years later, the rules changed. Players could dribble the ball as they ran. The basket problem got solved, too. A hoop with a net replaced each peach basket. The ball could swish right through. Basketball was a hit!

**NAME:** ____________________ **DATE:** ____________

**DIRECTIONS** Read "A New Game." Answer the questions.

**SCORE**

1. Why do you think basketball was a hit?

   Ⓐ It was a lot of work for the boys to play.

   Ⓑ It was fun to play and to watch.

   Ⓒ It had a lot of rules for playing.

2. Why is a hoop with a net better than a basket?

   Ⓐ The boys did not have to get the ball out of the basket.

   Ⓑ The boys did not get to rest as much.

   Ⓒ The boys did not have any more peach baskets.

3. Why do you think the rules changed?

   Ⓐ The players wanted to run with the ball.

   Ⓑ The players liked passing the ball.

   Ⓒ The players liked the peach basket.

4. What is another good title for this text?

   Ⓐ How to Dribble a Ball

   Ⓑ How to Solve a Problem

   Ⓒ The Beginnings of Basketball

1. ☺ 😐

2. ☺ 😐

3. ☺ 😐

4. ☺ 😐

___ / 4
Total

**NAME:** ______________________ **DATE:** ______________

SCORE
___/4

**Reread** "A New Game."

**Think about** how basketball and other sports are played.

**Write about** your favorite sport and tell how it is played.

NAME:________________________ DATE:________________

**DIRECTIONS** Read the text. Answer the questions.

SCORE

1. ☺ 😐
2. ☺ 😐
3. ☺ 😐
4. ☺ 😐

____ / 4
Total

Drew and Bree are on spring break. They are going on a hike in the mountains. They pack their lunches and gear into backpacks.

**1.** Where are Drew and Bree going?

(A) the mountains to ski

(B) the mountains to ice skate

(C) the mountains to hike

**2.** Why do they put their gear in backpacks?

(A) so they have their gear with them as they hike

(B) so they can leave their gear somewhere

(C) so they can fit the gear into the van

**3.** The word *backpack* is made of two words: *back* and *pack*. Which word is also made with two words?

(A) mailbox

(B) valentine

(C) pretzel

**4.** What does the word *gear* mean in this text?

(A) things they will leave in the car

(B) toys and games for the hike

(C) things they will need on the hike

**NAME:** ______________________ **DATE:** ______________

**DIRECTIONS** Read the text. Answer the questions.

SCORE

1. ☺ 😐

2. ☺ 😐

3. ☺ 😐

4. ☺ 😐

____ / 4
Total

Drew and Bree wear thick socks and sturdy shoes to hike. But Drew still gets a sore on one foot. They stop so he can put on a bandage.

**1.** Who gets a sore?

Ⓐ Drew

Ⓑ Bree

Ⓒ the socks

**2.** How will the bandage help?

Ⓐ It will pad the sore so it does not hurt.

Ⓑ It will keep the sore hidden.

Ⓒ It will make him walk more slowly.

**3.** Which word begins with the same sound as *thick*?

Ⓐ 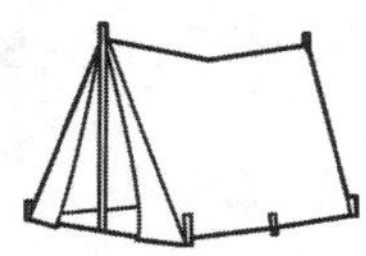

Ⓑ 

Ⓒ 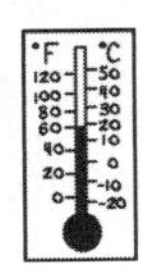

**4.** What does the word *sturdy* mean in this text?

Ⓐ thick

Ⓑ strong

Ⓒ light

**NAME:** ____________________ **DATE:** ______________

**DIRECTIONS** Read the text. Answer the questions.

**SCORE**

1. ☺ 😐
2. ☺ 😐
3. ☺ 😐
4. ☺ 😐

____ / 4
Total

Drew and Bree snack on trail mix on their hike. When Bree spills some, a chipmunk darts out and steals a peanut. Bree laughs and spills more trail mix.

**1.** Why do Bree and Drew eat trail mix?

Ⓐ because they found some

Ⓑ so they did not have to carry it

Ⓒ to have enough energy to keep hiking

**2.** Why do you think Bree spilled more trail mix?

Ⓐ to see if more chipmunks would come

Ⓑ because she did not want to eat it

Ⓒ because she tripped and fell

**3.** Which word ends with the same sound as *mix*?

Ⓐ sticks

Ⓑ plants

Ⓒ stamps

**4.** What does the word *darts* mean in this text?

Ⓐ sits

Ⓑ runs

Ⓒ swings

**NAME:** ______________________ **DATE:** ______________

# A Lunchtime Surprise

Bree and Drew are tired and hungry after three hours. They stop in a clearing and unpack their lunch. Their sandwiches and apples taste great. They start to clean up after they eat.

All of a sudden, Drew whispers, "Look!" There in the clearing is a deer and its fawn. Bree and Drew hold still until the deer leave.

Bree says, "That was the best!"

**NAME:** ____________________ **DATE:** ____________

**DIRECTIONS** Read "A Lunchtime Surprise." Answer the questions.

**1.** Why does Drew whisper?

- (A) so the deer won't be scared
- (B) so Bree won't be scared
- (C) so Bree won't eat

**2.** What is a fawn?

- (A) a mother deer
- (B) a baby deer
- (C) a father deer

**3.** Bree said, "That was the best!" What did she mean?

- (A) She was not hungry anymore.
- (B) She was ready to go home.
- (C) It was great to see the deer.

**4.** Which sentence best tells about this text?

- (A) Bree and Drew are hungry and have their lunch.
- (B) Bree and Drew have a picnic lunch and see deer.
- (C) Bree and Drew have the best day because they saw a chipmunk.

**SCORE**

1. ☺ 😐
2. ☺ 😐
3. ☺ 😐
4. ☺ 😐

____ / 4
**Total**

NAME: ______________________ DATE: ______________

SCORE

___ /4

**Reread** "A Lunchtime Surprise."

**Think about** when you go outside. What animals do you like to see? Have you been surprised by an animal?

**Write about** an animal you have seen.

NAME: ______________________ DATE: ______________

**DIRECTIONS** Read the text. Answer the questions.

SCORE

1. ☺ ☹
2. ☺ ☹
3. ☺ ☹
4. ☺ ☹

___ / 4
Total

Some dogs have important jobs. They are called *service dogs*. Some are trained to help blind or deaf people. These dogs are trained to keep their owners safe.

**1.** What kind of dog is this text about?

(A) pet dogs
(B) important dogs
(C) service dogs

**2.** What might a dog in this text do to help?

(A) walk someone across the street
(B) play with other dogs in the park
(C) chase animals away from a person

**3.** The word *important* has three syllables: *im-por-tant*. Which word has three syllables?

(A) thermometer
(B) watermelon
(C) umbrella

**4.** What does the word *trained* mean in this text?

(A) worked
(B) taught
(C) school

NAME: ____________________ DATE: ____________

**DIRECTIONS** Read the text. Answer the questions.

SCORE

1. ☺ 😐

2. ☺ 😐

3. ☺ 😐

4. ☺ 😐

____ / 4
Total

Some service dogs help deaf people. Did the doorbell just ring? This dog will touch its owner. It will even wake up a person if an alarm goes off.

**1.** What can a service dog do?

Ⓐ sing

Ⓑ ring a doorbell

Ⓒ help a deaf person

**2.** How does the dog tell a deaf person something?

Ⓐ It barks loudly at the person.

Ⓑ It touches the person.

Ⓒ It jumps onto the person.

**3.** Which word is spelled correctly?

Ⓐ person

Ⓑ prson

Ⓒ persen

**4.** What does *alarm* mean in this text?

Ⓐ a clock that ticks loudly

Ⓑ a radio or television program

Ⓒ a buzzer or bell that warns

 

NAME:____________________ DATE:______________

**DIRECTIONS** Read the text. Answer the questions.

Some service dogs help people who use a wheelchair. They can turn lights on and off. They can pick up a book. They can even open and close doors.

**1.** What do the service dogs do?

Ⓐ They help people who cannot get around easily.

Ⓑ They help people who want to train a dog.

Ⓒ They help people get well.

**2.** Which sentence is **not** true?

Ⓐ Service dogs can turn lights on and off.

Ⓑ Service dogs can use a wheelchair.

Ⓒ Service dogs can pick up a book.

**3.** The word *wheelchair* is made of two words: *wheel* and *chair.* Which word is also made of two words?

Ⓐ kangaroo

Ⓑ helicopter

Ⓒ sailboat

**4.** What does the word *service* mean in this text?

Ⓐ playful

Ⓑ helpful

Ⓒ careful

**SCORE**

1. ☺ 😐

2. ☺ 😐

3. ☺ 😐

4. ☺ 😐

____ / 4 Total

NAME:______________________ DATE:____________

# Dog Heroes

Has there been an earthquake? Did a bad storm hit? Did a hiker get lost on a mountain? That is when some dogs go to work. They are called *search and rescue dogs*. Dogs have a much better sense of smell than people have. They have been trained to use those noses. Dogs have found people buried under snow or buildings. They are real heroes!

**NAME:** ______________________ **DATE:** ______________

**DIRECTIONS** Read "Dog Heroes." Answer the questions.

**SCORE**

1. ☺ 😐
2. ☺ 😐
3. ☺ 😐
4. ☺ 😐

____ / 4
Total

**1.** What does *search and rescue* mean?

- Ⓐ to dig up things or people
- Ⓑ to help people get around
- Ⓒ to look for and save people

**2.** When does a search and rescue dog go to work?

- Ⓐ when their owners have time
- Ⓑ when people are lost or missing
- Ⓒ when they are trained

**3.** Why are dogs good at searches?

- Ⓐ They are strong and work hard.
- Ⓑ They can smell things that are buried.
- Ⓒ They like to hunt and run.

**4.** What is another good title for this text?

- Ⓐ Dogs on the Run!
- Ⓑ Dogs and People!
- Ⓒ Dogs to the Rescue!

**NAME:** ______________________ **DATE:** ______________

SCORE

___ / 4

**Reread** "Dog Heroes."

**Think about** how dogs help people. How would you like a dog to help you? Would it clean up your room? Do tricks that make you laugh? Keep you warm at night?

**Write about** what you would like a dog to do.

 

**NAME:** ____________________ **DATE:** ______________

**DIRECTIONS** Read the text. Answer the questions.

SCORE

1. ☺ 😐
2. ☺ 😐
3. ☺ 😐
4. ☺ 😐

____ / 4
Total

Chan and Ella are at the beach. They want to see lots of fish. Mom says she will teach them to snorkel. Then they can look for fish underwater.

**1.** Who will teach Chan and Ella to snorkel?

Ⓐ the beach
Ⓑ the fish
Ⓒ Mom

**2.** Why will they learn to snorkel?

Ⓐ so they can see fish swimming nearby
Ⓑ so they can swim faster with flippers
Ⓒ so they can play in the water

**3.** Which word rhymes with *fish*?

Ⓐ shell
Ⓑ peach
Ⓒ dish

**4.** What does *lots* mean?

Ⓐ some
Ⓑ many
Ⓒ a few

**NAME:** ____________________ **DATE:** ____________

**DIRECTIONS** Read the text. Answer the questions.

SCORE

1. ☺ 😐

2. ☺ 😐

3. ☺ 😐

4. ☺ 😐

___ / 4
Total

Chan and Ella get into the water. They float on their stomachs. The flippers help them move. The mask lets them see things. The snorkel tube lets them breathe.

**1.** What helps Chan and Ella move?

Ⓐ the masks

Ⓑ the waves

Ⓒ the flippers

**2.** How do they breathe?

Ⓐ through the snorkel tubes

Ⓑ through the masks

Ⓒ by taking breaks

**3.** Which word is spelled incorrectly?

Ⓐ move

Ⓑ boot

Ⓒ wadr

**4.** What does *mask* mean in this text?

Ⓐ something that covers the mouth

Ⓑ something that covers the hair

Ⓒ something that covers the nose and eyes

 

**NAME:** ____________________ **DATE:** ______________

**DIRECTIONS** Read the text. Answer the questions.

Snorkeling is easy to learn. Chan and Ella see fish in different colors and shapes. Some are striped. Some have spots. Some are long and thin.

**1.** Which sentence is true?

Ⓐ Chan and Ella do not like snorkeling.

Ⓑ Chan and Ella learn to snorkel quickly.

Ⓒ Chan and Ella want to quit snorkeling.

**2.** What kind of fish did they see?

Ⓐ striped and spotted

Ⓑ big with long fins

Ⓒ fast and slow

**3.** Which word starts with the same sounds as *striped*?

Ⓐ some

Ⓑ snorkeling

Ⓒ string

**4.** What is the opposite of *long and thin*?

Ⓐ short and fat

Ⓑ tall and skinny

Ⓒ small and thick

**SCORE**

1. ☺ 😐

2. ☺ 😐

3. ☺ 😐

4. ☺ 😐

____ / 4
**Total**

NAME:____________________ DATE:_______________

# Shark!

Chan and Ella take a boat out to a coral reef. A reef looks like a forest under the sea. The coral looks like colorful plants. They are really tiny sea animals. There are lots of fish in the reef. Chan and Ella see fish with odd names like chub and grunt. But the best comes last. A small blacktip reef shark glides by.

**NAME:** ______________________ **DATE:** ______________

**DIRECTIONS** Read "Shark!" Answer the questions.

**SCORE**

1. ☺ ☹
2. ☺ ☹
3. ☺ ☹
4. ☺ ☹

___ / 4
Total

**1.** What sentence is true?

Ⓐ A coral reef has no plants.
Ⓑ Corals are small sea animals.
Ⓒ Fish keep away from reefs.

**2.** How do you think the blacktip reef shark got its name?

Ⓐ Its fins have black tips. It swims around reefs.
Ⓑ Its nose has a tip. It swims deep in the sea.
Ⓒ Its has black eyes. It swims in the waves.

**3.** What does the word *odd* mean in this text?

Ⓐ funny
Ⓑ short
Ⓒ pretty

**4.** What is another good title for this text?

Ⓐ Swimming on the Beach
Ⓑ A Boat Ride
Ⓒ Snorkeling at a Reef

**NAME:** ______________________ **DATE:** ______________

SCORE
___ / 4

**Reread** "Shark!"

**Think about** different fish. If you could name a fish, what would you name it?

**Write about** what you would call it and why.

**NAME:** ____________________ **DATE:** ______________

**DIRECTIONS** Read the text. Answer the questions.

**SCORE**

1. ☺ 😐
2. ☺ 😐
3. ☺ 😐
4. ☺ 😐

___ / 4 Total

A hurricane is a huge storm. It begins over the ocean. The winds blow in a circle. The winds can blow up to 200 miles per hour. It rains hard.

**1.** What is a hurricane?

(A) a storm that starts over land

(B) a storm that starts over water

(C) a storm that starts over islands

**2.** Which sentence is true about a hurricane?

(A) Strong winds blow in a circle.

(B) Light winds blow across the ocean.

(C) Strong winds can blow 300 miles per hour.

**3.** The word *hurricane* has three syllables: *hur-ri-cane*. Which word also has three syllables?

(A) alligator

(B) hammer

(C) grasshopper

**4.** What word means the same as *ocean*?

(A) lake

(B) island

(C) sea

**NAME:** ____________________ **DATE:** ______________

**DIRECTIONS** Read the text. Answer the questions.

SCORE

1. ☺ 😐

2. ☺ 😐

3. ☺ 😐

4. ☺ 😐

____ / 4
Total

The center of a hurricane is called the *eye*. The winds do not blow as hard in the eye. It does not rain as much.

**1.** What is the *eye* of a hurricane?

Ⓐ the outer edge of the storm

Ⓑ the area where the storm starts

Ⓒ the area in the middle of the storm

**2.** What is it like in the eye?

Ⓐ The storm is quieter.

Ⓑ The storm is windier.

Ⓒ The storm is rainier.

**3.** Which word rhymes with *wind*?

Ⓐ grinned

Ⓑ whine

Ⓒ wide

**4.** What does the word *hard* mean in this text?

Ⓐ mean

Ⓑ strongly

Ⓒ fast

 

**NAME:** ______________________ **DATE:** ______________

**DIRECTIONS** Read the text. Answer the questions.

The winds in a hurricane push the water around. Giant waves form. The sea level can get very high. This is called a *storm surge*.

**1.** What happens in a storm surge?

Ⓐ The waves and sea level get high.

Ⓑ The waves get smaller in the eye.

Ⓒ The waves make more wind and rain.

**2.** What pushes the waves in a hurricane?

Ⓐ water

Ⓑ wind

Ⓒ rain

**3.** Which word ends with the same sound as *surge*?

Ⓐ church

Ⓑ match

Ⓒ bridge

**4.** What does *giant* mean in this text?

Ⓐ strong

Ⓑ huge

Ⓒ fast

**SCORE**

1. ☺ 😐

2. ☺ 😐

3. ☺ 😐

4. ☺ 😐

____ / 4
**Total**

NAME:______________________ DATE:______________

# A Hurricane on Land

Is a hurricane coming? Do you live near the ocean? Then you may need to leave home until the storm ends. The strong winds can tear up trees. The rain can cause flooding. The sea level may rise with the storm surge. Boats can get tossed around by the waves. The beach may get worn away. Be sure to go somewhere safe if a hurricane is coming.

**NAME:** ______________________ **DATE:** ______________

**DIRECTIONS** Read "A Hurricane on Land." Answer the questions.

**SCORE**

1. ☺ 😐
2. ☺ 😐
3. ☺ 😐
4. ☺ 😐

____ / 4
Total

**1.** What kind of place would be safe in a hurricane?

(A) a big house by the beach

(B) a house away from the beach

(C) a park near the ocean

**2.** Why do some people have to leave home?

(A) A hurricane keeps people at their jobs.

(B) It may not be safe during a hurricane.

(C) The hurricane is fun to watch.

**3.** Which sentence is true?

(A) People should watch the storm come in.

(B) People should swim in the big waves.

(C) People should tie down their boats.

**4.** What is the main idea of this text?

(A) A hurricane can be unsafe when it hits land.

(B) A hurricane can be shown on TV.

(C) A hurricane moves faster across land.

**NAME:** ______________________ **DATE:** ______________

SCORE

___ / 4

**Reread** "A Hurricane on Land."

**Think about** what a beach looks like before a big storm. What would it look like after a big storm?

**Write about** what a beach is like after a storm.

NAME: ______________________ DATE: ______________

**DIRECTIONS** Read the text. Answer the questions.

SCORE

1. ☺ 😐
2. ☺ 😐
3. ☺ 😐
4. ☺ 😐

____ / 4
Total

"Your birthday is Saturday, Tan. What would you like to do?" asks Papa.

"I would like to ride on a train. No, I would like to ride on an elephant. And maybe ride a horse," says Tan.

**1.** Why is Papa asking Tan about Saturday?

Ⓐ Papa wants to bake Tan a cake.

Ⓑ Papa wants to take Tan shopping.

Ⓒ Papa wants to plan Tan's birthday.

**2.** How many animals does Tan want to ride?

Ⓐ one

Ⓑ two

Ⓒ three

**3.** Which word has the same vowel sound as *train*?

Ⓐ cage

Ⓑ card

Ⓒ caught

**4.** What does *maybe* mean?

Ⓐ not for sure

Ⓑ yes

Ⓒ tomorrow

**NAME:** ____________________ **DATE:** ____________

**DIRECTIONS** Read the text. Answer the questions.

SCORE

1. ☺ ☹

2. ☺ ☹

3. ☺ ☹

4. ☺ ☹

___ / 4
Total

Pop says, "A horse ride would be fun. What else would you like to do for your birthday?"

Tan says, "I would like to play with butterflies and birds. Could I pet lizards, too?"

**1.** Who are the main characters in this text?

(A) Tan and Papa
(B) butterflies and birds
(C) lizards

**2.** What does Tan want to pet?

(A) butterflies
(B) birds
(C) lizards

**3.** What rhymes with *ride*?

(A) tied
(B) ripe
(C) slip

**4.** What does *pet* mean in this text?

(A) touch or pat lightly
(B) an animal kept in the home
(C) hold onto

 

**NAME:** ______________________ **DATE:** ______________

**DIRECTIONS** Read the text. Answer the questions.

**SCORE**

1. ☺ 😐

2. ☺ 😐

3. ☺ 😐

4. ☺ 😐

____ / 4
Total

"That is a lot to do on your birthday," Papa says. "I hope we have the time."

"I thought of more to do," says Tan. "Could I see a shark or turtle? And have a picnic, too?"

**1.** Who is Tan?

Ⓐ Mom

Ⓑ a turtle

Ⓒ the son

**2.** Why do you think Tan wants to do so much?

Ⓐ He wants to have fun.

Ⓑ He wants his Papa to plan the day.

Ⓒ He wants to go to the movies.

**3.** Which word has the same vowel sound as *too*?

Ⓐ moon

Ⓑ son

Ⓒ cold

**4.** What does *picnic* mean?

Ⓐ an outdoor table

Ⓑ an outdoor party

Ⓒ an outdoor meal

NAME:______________________ DATE:______________

# The Birthday Surprise

Tan's birthday is here! Papa has a surprise trip. Tan rides a horse on the carousel. He rides an elephant and rides on the zoo train, too. Butterflies land on Tan in the butterfly garden. A parrot talks to Papa in the bird house. Tan pets a lizard and a turtle in the reptile house. After a picnic, they see a tiger. What a great birthday!

**NAME:** ____________________ **DATE:** ____________

**DIRECTIONS** Read "The Birthday Surprise." Answer the questions.

**SCORE**

1. ☺ 😐
2. ☺ 😐
3. ☺ 😐
4. ☺ 😐

___ / 4
Total

**1.** What does *reptile house* mean?

Ⓐ a place where animals like lizards live

Ⓑ a place where animals like bears live

Ⓒ a place where animals like birds live

**2.** Where do Papa and Tan go?

Ⓐ the zoo

Ⓑ the park

Ⓒ the train station

**3.** When do they have the picnic?

Ⓐ before Tan rides the train

Ⓑ before Tan pets a turtle

Ⓒ before they see a tiger

**4.** What is another good title for this text?

Ⓐ A Birthday Picnic

Ⓑ A Birthday at the Zoo

Ⓒ A Birthday Ride

**NAME:** ______________________ **DATE:** ______________

SCORE

___ / 4

**Reread** "The Birthday Surprise."

**Think about** your next birthday. Would you like to have a party at home? Maybe you would like to go somewhere. Would you like to celebrate with your family? Would you like to have friends come over?

**Write about** what you would like to do on your birthday.

NAME: ______________________ DATE: ______________

**DIRECTIONS** Read the text. Answer the questions.

Have you ever lost a pet? There are things you can do to search for a lost pet. You can look around where you live. You can put up signs about your missing pet. You can put out food it likes.

**1.** What is this text mostly about?

(A) food pets like

(B) how to take care of a pet

(C) finding a lost pet

**2.** What is **not** a way to search for a lost pet?

(A) look around

(B) look in a book

(C) put up signs

**3.** Which word ends with the same sound as *search*?

(A) brush

(B) chimney

(C) watch

**4.** What is the opposite of *missing*?

(A) found

(B) lost

(C) skip

**SCORE**

1. ☺ 😐

2. ☺ 😐

3. ☺ 😐

4. ☺ 😐

____ / 4 Total

**NAME:** ____________________ **DATE:** ____________

**DIRECTIONS** Read the text. Answer the questions.

**SCORE**

1. ☺ ☹
2. ☺ ☹
3. ☺ ☹
4. ☺ ☹

____ / 4
Total

Some people have been trained to look for lost pets. They are called *pet detectives*. They will ask lots of questions about your pet. They will want a picture of your pet.

**1.** Why would someone use a pet detective?

- (A) because they like detectives
- (B) because they want to learn about pets
- (C) because they need help finding their pet

**2.** What kind of questions would pet detectives ask?

- (A) questions about the weather
- (B) questions about your pet
- (C) questions about your favorite things

**3.** Which word is spelled correctly?

- (A) traned
- (B) trained
- (C) chrained

**4.** What sentence uses the word *train* in the same way as in this text?

- (A) The train traveled along the tracks.
- (B) The bride's train flowed behind her dress.
- (C) Kim trained to run in a race.

 

**NAME:** ______________________ **DATE:** ______________

**DIRECTIONS** Read the text. Answer the questions.

SCORE

1. ☺ ☹
2. ☺ ☹
3. ☺ ☹
4. ☺ ☹

___ / 4 Total

Some pet detectives own a helpful dog. They have the dog sniff things the lost pet used. The dog follows a trail of those smells. This dog is called a *tracking dog*.

**1.** Why do some pet detectives own dogs?

Ⓐ Dogs are fun to own.
Ⓑ Some dogs like to run and play.
Ⓒ The dogs help them do their job.

**2.** What work does the tracking dog do?

Ⓐ It sniffs at things.
Ⓑ It tracks lost pets.
Ⓒ It plays with pets.

**3.** Which word rhymes with *smells*?

Ⓐ bowls
Ⓑ hills
Ⓒ bells

**4.** What does *tracking* mean in this text?

Ⓐ the dog follows something
Ⓑ the dog leads other dogs
Ⓒ the dog likes to play with other dogs–

NAME:_________________________ DATE:_______________

# Keeping Pets Safe

Some tracking dogs find a lost pet quickly. Sometimes they lose the trail. Someone may put a pet in a car. Sometimes a pet is taken inside a building. Then the trail is lost. Some pets get hit by a car. You can help keep your pet safe. You can have the vet put a tiny chip in a dog or cat. That chip tells who the animal belongs to. But the best thing to do is to keep the pet in the house or yard.

NAME: ______________________ DATE: ______________

**DIRECTIONS** Read "Keeping Pets Safe." Answer the questions.

**1.** Why might a pet get hit by a car?

- (A) It is running in the street.
- (B) It is looking for food.
- (C) It finds a bone.

**2.** Where can you get a chip put in your pet?

- (A) at the pet store
- (B) at the vet's office
- (C) at home

**3.** How can you keep your pet safe?

- (A) train it to stay out of cars
- (B) keep it in the house or yard
- (C) feed it chips

**4.** What is the main idea?

- (A) It is important to keep your pet safe.
- (B) It is important to have a pet.
- (C) It is important to train your pet.

SCORE

1. ☺ 😐
2. ☺ 😐
3. ☺ 😐
4. ☺ 😐

____ / 4
Total

**NAME:** ______________________ **DATE:** ________________

SCORE
___ / 4

**Reread** "Keeping Pets Safe."

**Think about** things that can be done to keep a pet safe.

**Write about** how to keep a pet safe.

 

**NAME:** ______________________ **DATE:** ______________

**DIRECTIONS** Read the text. Answer the questions.

Maddy and Pat love when spring comes. They go to see their grandparents each weekend. They work on the farm. But they have a lot of fun, too.

**1.** Where do the grandparents live?

(A) in the town
(B) on a farm
(C) with Maddy and Pat

**2.** When do Maddy and Pat see their grandparents?

(A) on weekdays in the spring
(B) one week in the spring
(C) on weekends in the spring

**3.** The word *weekend* is made of two words: *week* and *end*. Which word is also made of two words?

(A) picture
(B) turkey
(C) wheelchair

**4.** What does *spring* mean in this text?

(A) the time of year after summer
(B) the time of year before fall
(C) the time of year after winter

**SCORE**

1. ☺ 😐
2. ☺ 😐
3. ☺ 😐
4. ☺ 😐

____ / 4
Total

NAME: ______________________ DATE: ______________

**DIRECTIONS** Read the text. Answer the questions.

SCORE

1. ☺ ☹

2. ☺ ☹

3. ☺ ☹

4. ☺ ☹

____ / 4
Total

Many animals are born in the spring. Sheep have baby lambs. Goats have their kids. Cows have calves, and horses have their foals. Maddy and Pat get to pet them all.

**1.** Who pets the baby animals?

Ⓐ sheep and goats
Ⓑ cows and horses
Ⓒ Maddy and Pat

**2.** What are baby goats called?

Ⓐ kids
Ⓑ foals
Ⓒ Billy

**3.** What word rhymes with *foal*?

Ⓐ cold
Ⓑ hole
Ⓒ coat

**4.** To whom does *their* refer in the third sentence?

Ⓐ all the animals
Ⓑ goats
Ⓒ kids

 

**NAME:** ____________________ **DATE:** ______________

**DIRECTIONS** Read the text. Answer the questions.

SCORE

1. ☺ 😐
2. ☺ 😐
3. ☺ 😐
4. ☺ 😐

___ / 4
Total

Maddy and Pat pick ripe strawberries in May. They fill up boxes of them. They have shortcake for dessert. They help Grandmother make jam. They eat as much as they pick!

**1.** Whom do Maddy and Pat help?

Ⓐ shortcake

Ⓑ Mom

Ⓒ Grandmother

**2.** What kind of dessert do they have?

Ⓐ blueberry shortcake

Ⓑ strawberry shortcake

Ⓒ ice cream and strawberries

**3.** The word *strawberry* means one. The word *strawberries* means more than one. What word means more than one *pony*?

Ⓐ ponys

Ⓑ ponies

Ⓒ pones

**4.** What does the word *ripe* mean in this text?

Ⓐ fresh and green

Ⓑ soft and mushy

Ⓒ ready to be picked

**NAME:** ______________________ **DATE:** ______________

# Taking a Ride

One day, Grandfather tells Maddy and Pat to come outside for a surprise. Two ponies and a horse stand quietly by the fence. Each pony has a brand new saddle on it. Grandfather says, "You have worked hard. These are for you! Get on the ponies, and let's go for a ride." They all ride until sunset.

Then Grandfather says, "Time for all of us to eat. Let's go home."

**NAME:** ______________________ **DATE:** ______________

**DIRECTIONS** Read "Taking a Ride." Answer the questions.

**SCORE**

1. ☺ 😐
2. ☺ 😐
3. ☺ 😐
4. ☺ 😐

___ / 4
Total

**1.** What was the surprise?

- (A) Maddy and Pat got to play in the barn.
- (B) Maddy and Pat got to ride their own ponies.
- (C) Maddy and Pat got to work hard.

**2.** What is a *saddle*?

- (A) a sad man who rides a horse
- (B) a seat for someone to ride on a horse
- (C) a type of spoon tha- feeds hay to horses

**3.** Why do they go home?

- (A) The people and animals need dinner.
- (B) The barn needs to be cleaned up.
- (C) Grandmother called them in.

**4.** What is another good title for this text?

- (A) The Surprise Ponies
- (B) The Surprise Dinner
- (C) Working on the Farm

**NAME:** ______________________ **DATE:** ______________

SCORE

___/4

**Reread** "Taking a Ride."

**Think about** what it would be like to have a pony. What would you name it? What would it look like?

**Write about** a pony you would like to ride or have.

**NAME:** ______________________ **DATE:** ______________

**DIRECTIONS** Read the text. Answer the questions.

SCORE

1. ☺ 😐

2. ☺ 😐

3. ☺ 😐

4. ☺ 😐

___ / 4
Total

A turkey vulture is a useful bird. You could call it a garbage collector. It does not kill. It lets others do that job. A lion may kill a deer and just eat part of it. The vulture eats all that is left but the bones.

**1.** Why would you call a turkey vulture a *garbage collector*?

- (A) It eats the bones of animals.
- (B) It cleans up the mess of dead animals.
- (C) It kills deer and lions.

**2.** What does the turkey vulture eat?

- (A) bones and skins of lions
- (B) garbage left by picnickers
- (C) everything but the bones

**3.** Which word begins with the same sound as *vulture*?

- (A) turkey
- (B) umbrella
- (C) vase

**4.** What does the word *useful* mean in this text?

- (A) helpful
- (B) careful
- (C) awful

**NAME:** ______________________ **DATE:** ______________

**DIRECTIONS** Read the text. Answer the questions.

SCORE

1. ☺ 😐

2. ☺ 😐

3. ☺ 😐

4. ☺ 😐

____ / 4
Total

The turkey vulture has a red, bald head. It has to put its head inside the dead animal to eat. Its food would stick to its feathers. That bald head helps keep this big bird clean.

**1.** How does this kind of bird eat?

- (A) It pulls food out with its head.
- (B) It tears food out with its feet.
- (C) It pulls food out with its claws.

**2.** Why do you think it is called a *turkey* vulture?

- (A) It eats like a turkey.
- (B) It likes to eat turkeys.
- (C) Its head looks like a turkey head.

**3.** Which word rhymes with *clean*?

- (A) bean
- (B) beak
- (C) belt

**4.** What does *bald* mean in this text?

- (A) without ears
- (B) without feathers
- (C) without hair

**NAME:** ______________________ **DATE:** ______________

**DIRECTIONS** Read the text. Answer the questions.

**SCORE**

1. ☺ 😐

2. ☺ 😐

3. ☺ 😐

4. ☺ 😐

____ / 4
Total

Turkey vultures fly low. They are looking for food. They can see and smell well. They watch for other vultures flying down toward the ground. They will follow the others to dinner!

**1.** How do turkey vultures look for food?

Ⓐ They fly at night and hunt for mice to eat.

Ⓑ They fly and use their sense of sight and smell.

Ⓒ They fly and watch for animals that kill.

**2.** What helps vultures find food?

Ⓐ their sense of sight

Ⓑ their sense of taste

Ⓒ their sense of hearing

**3.** Which word starts with the same sounds as *flying*?

Ⓐ flower

Ⓑ fan

Ⓒ feather

**4.** What does the word *follow* mean?

Ⓐ go before

Ⓑ go next to

Ⓒ go behind

**NAME:** ____________________ **DATE:** ____________

# Dinnertime!

A turkey vulture may eat a lot. That can be a problem if a snake wants to eat the vulture for dinner. The bird may be too heavy to fly away. So it does something a bit gross. It throws up some food. Some people think that this is so the vulture will get lighter. Others think this is so the snake now has a different dinner. Smart bird!

**NAME:** ______________________ **DATE:** ______________

**DIRECTIONS** Read "Dinnertime!" Answer the questions.

**SCORE**

1. What might be a problem for a turkey vulture?

   Ⓐ eating too little food
   Ⓑ eating old food
   Ⓒ eating too much food

2. What might a snake do to a vulture?

   Ⓐ kill and eat it
   Ⓑ share its food
   Ⓒ scare it away

3. What does the word *gross* mean in this text?

   Ⓐ not smart
   Ⓑ yucky
   Ⓒ mean

4. Why does the text say a vulture is a *smart bird*?

   Ⓐ It knows how to keep safe from snakes.
   Ⓑ It knows how to eat dead meat.
   Ⓒ It knows how to throw up.

1. ☺ 😐
2. ☺ 😐
3. ☺ 😐
4. ☺ 😐

____ / 4
**Total**

**NAME:** ______________________ **DATE:** ______________

SCORE

___ / 4

**Reread** "Dinnertime!"

**Think about** all you know about the turkey vulture.

**Write about** the things you learned about the bird. Make a list.

 

NAME: ______________________ DATE: ______________

**DIRECTIONS** Read the text. Answer the questions.

SCORE

1. ☺ 😐
2. ☺ 😐
3. ☺ 😐
4. ☺ 😐

____ / 4
Total

Mara and Joe are on a field trip. Their class is at the Cave of the Winds. They will go very deep in the cave on the tour. It will be so dark that they will need to carry a lantern to see.

**1.** Where is the class going?

Ⓐ on a bus trip
Ⓑ on a cave tour
Ⓒ on a hike

**2.** Why will it be dark on the tour?

Ⓐ They will be deep under the ground.
Ⓑ They will be on the tour at night.
Ⓒ They will be walking without lights.

**3.** Which word rhymes with *field*?

Ⓐ sealed
Ⓑ filed
Ⓒ held

**4.** What is another word for *lantern*?

Ⓐ cave
Ⓑ dark
Ⓒ light

NAME: ______________________ DATE: ______________

**DIRECTIONS** Read the text. Answer the questions.

SCORE

1. ☺ ☹

2. ☺ ☹

3. ☺ ☹

4. ☺ ☹

___ / 4
Total

Mara and Joe get a surprise. A ringtail cat darts past them. It is part of the raccoon family. Their guide says that it mostly hides. The guide also talks about the bats that live in the cave.

**1.** Who is in the cave with Mara and Joe?

Ⓐ their mom
Ⓑ their family
Ⓒ a guide

**2.** What do they learn about?

Ⓐ bats in the cave
Ⓑ insects in the cave
Ⓒ animals in the cave

**3.** Which word is spelled correctly?

Ⓐ kave
Ⓑ cave
Ⓒ cav

**4.** What does *mostly* mean in this text?

Ⓐ all of the time
Ⓑ a lot
Ⓒ not often

**NAME:** ______________________ **DATE:** ______________

**DIRECTIONS** Read the text. Answer the questions.

Joe and Mara walk carefully through the cave. Some of the trail is wet and slippery. They have to squeeze through some narrow places. It is dark and still. The only light comes from the lanterns.

**1.** Which does **not** tell where Joe and Mara are?

- (A) on a trail
- (B) outside
- (C) in a cave

**2.** Why do they walk carefully?

- (A) The cave is pretty to see.
- (B) The trail is slippery and dark.
- (C) The trail is long.

**3.** Which word has the same ending sound as *squeeze*?

- (A) sips
- (B) sneeze
- (C) cups

**4.** What does *slippery* mean in this text?

- (A) dark
- (B) safe
- (C) slick

**SCORE**

1. ☺ 😐

2. ☺ 😐

3. ☺ 😐

4. ☺ 😐

____ / 4 Total

**NAME:**____________________________ **DATE:**________________

# Frozen Sights

The class sees rocks of all kinds of shapes. They see big things that look like icicles. The ones that hang down are called *stalactites* (stuh-LAK-tahyts). The ones that come up from the ground are called *stalagmites* (stuh-LAG-mahyts). Some walls look like frozen waterfalls. Mara and Joe are glad they have worn their coats! They like the tour. But they are glad to get back to the sunshine.

**NAME:** ____________________ **DATE:** ______________

**DIRECTIONS** Read "Frozen Sights." Answer the questions.

**SCORE**

1. ☺ ☹
2. ☺ ☹
3. ☺ ☹
4. ☺ ☹

___ / 4 Total

**1.** Why are Mara and Joe glad they have their coats?

- (A) It is dark in the cave.
- (B) It is cold in the cave.
- (C) It is quiet in the cave.

**2.** What does a stalagmite look like?

- (A) a huge icicle on the ground
- (B) a huge icicle on the ceiling
- (C) a frozen waterfall

**3.** How do you think Mara and Joe feel at the end of the tour?

- (A) They wish they had not seen the bats.
- (B) They wish they were still in the cold and dark.
- (C) They are happy that they saw the cave.

**4.** What does the title "Frozen Sights" mean?

- (A) They saw things in the cave that looked frozen.
- (B) They saw things that used to be frozen.
- (C) They saw dripping icicles in the cave.

**NAME:** ____________________ **DATE:** ____________

SCORE
___ / 4

**Reread** "Frozen Sights."

**Think about** what Mara and Joe saw in the cave.

**Write about** what you would like to see and do in a cave. Then, write about what you would **not** want to see or do in a cave. Make two lists.

 

**NAME:** ____________________ **DATE:** ______________

**DIRECTIONS** Read the text. Answer the questions.

SCORE

1. ☺ 😐
2. ☺ 😐
3. ☺ 😐
4. ☺ 😐

____ / 4
Total

Years ago, there were captains of ships with one goal. They wanted to steal all the gold they could. Some kings and queens asked the captains to steal. They were expected to share the treasures.

**1.** What did the ship captains want to do?

Ⓐ sail the seas

Ⓑ get rich by stealing

Ⓒ explore the seas

**2.** What did some kings and queens want?

Ⓐ to get some of the stolen things

Ⓑ to learn about the seas

Ⓒ to get captains to fight for them

**3.** The word *captain* has two syllables: *cap-tain*. Which word also has two syllables?

Ⓐ heard

Ⓑ head

Ⓒ hello

**4.** Who does *they* refer to in this text?

Ⓐ the captains

Ⓑ kings and queens

Ⓒ the treasure

**NAME:** ____________________ **DATE:** ______________

**DIRECTIONS** Read the text. Answer the questions.

SCORE

1. ☺ 😐
2. ☺ 😐
3. ☺ 😐
4. ☺ 😐

___ / 4
Total

Edward Teach was a scary man. He had a long, black beard. He liked to wear several pistols. He put knives in his belt. He captured many ships. As Blackbeard, Edward Teach is known as the most famous pirate.

**1.** Which does the text **not** tell us about Edward Teach?

Ⓐ He was famous.
Ⓑ He was Blackbeard.
Ⓒ He was a king.

**2.** Where did he keep knives?

Ⓐ in his pockets
Ⓑ in his belt
Ⓒ in his jacket

**3.** Which word rhymes with the word *known*?

Ⓐ clown
Ⓑ gown
Ⓒ throne

**4.** What does *pistols* mean in this text?

Ⓐ ships
Ⓑ guns
Ⓒ pirates

 

**NAME:** ____________________ **DATE:** ______________

**DIRECTIONS** Read the text. Answer the questions.

A sloop was one of the best ships for a pirate. It was not the biggest ship. But it was fast. This helped pirates win battles. The pirates could attack and get away quickly.

**1.** Why was a sloop a good ship for a pirate?

Ⓐ It was one of the biggest ships.

Ⓑ It held lots of treasure chests.

Ⓒ It was fast during a pirate attack.

**2.** When would a sloop **not** be a good ship for a pirate?

Ⓐ when the pirates wanted lots of room

Ⓑ when the pirates wanted to go to shore

Ⓒ when the pirates wanted to win fights

**3.** Which word has the same vowel sound as *sloop*?

Ⓐ book

Ⓑ roof

Ⓒ foot

**4.** What is a *ship*?

Ⓐ a boat

Ⓑ a pirate

Ⓒ a battle

**SCORE**

1. ☺ 😐

2. ☺ 😐

3. ☺ 😐

4. ☺ 😐

___ / 4
Total

**NAME:** ____________________ **DATE:** ______________

# A Different Pirate

Mary Read was an unlucky woman. It was hard for her to find work. So she fought in a war dressed like a man. She got married, but her husband died. She sailed away, and her ship was attacked by pirates. Mary chose to stay and be a pirate. Later, these pirates were caught. Mary went to prison.

**Mary Read**

 

**NAME:** ______________________ **DATE:** ______________

**DIRECTIONS** Read "A Different Pirate." Answer the questions.

**SCORE**

1. ☺ 😐
2. ☺ 😐
3. ☺ 😐
4. ☺ 😐

___ / 4
Total

**1.** Which is true?

Ⓐ Only men were pirates.

Ⓑ Only women were pirates.

Ⓒ Men and women were pirates.

**2.** Why did Mary dress like a man?

Ⓐ so she could sail on a ship

Ⓑ so she could fight in a war

Ⓒ so she could get married

**3.** Why do you think Mary was put in prison?

Ⓐ Mary was poor.

Ⓑ Pirates sailed in ships.

Ⓒ Mary was a pirate and pirates stole things.

**4.** What is another good title for this text?

Ⓐ An Unlucky Woman

Ⓑ A Lucky Woman

Ⓒ A Mean Woman

**NAME:** ______________________ **DATE:** ______________

SCORE
___ / 4

**Reread** "A Different Pirate."

**Think about** what you have read about pirates.

**Write about** one day in the life of a pirate.

 

NAME: ____________________ DATE: ______________

**DIRECTIONS** Read the text. Answer the questions.

SCORE

1. ☺ 😐
2. ☺ 😐
3. ☺ 😐
4. ☺ 😐

____ / 4 Total

Nick wakes up early on Saturday. "Get up!" he says to Fran. "The amusement park opens in two hours. I want to be first in line at the ticket booth!"

Fran pulls back her covers. She is already dressed!

**1.** Where are Fran and Nick going?

- (A) to an animal park
- (B) to a playground in the park
- (C) to an amusement park

**2.** Why do you think Fran was already dressed?

- (A) She was excited about the day.
- (B) She stayed up all night.
- (C) She wanted to stay in bed.

**3.** The word *amusement* has three syllables: *a-muse-ment*. Which word also has three syllables?

- (A) wagon
- (B) fisherman
- (C) football

**4.** What is the opposite of *early*?

- (A) late
- (B) now
- (C) soon

**NAME:** ____________________ **DATE:** ____________

**DIRECTIONS** Read the text. Answer the questions.

**SCORE**

1. ☺ 😐

2. ☺ 😐

3. ☺ 😐

4. ☺ 😐

____ / 4 Total

Nick and Fran hurry to the Twister. They want to ride before the roller coaster lines get long. They cling to the car as it climbs to the top and waits. Then it twists and turns as it races the track. Whee!

**1.** Where do Nick and Fran go first?

Ⓐ the roller coaster

Ⓑ the car

Ⓒ the track

**2.** Why do Nick and Fran hurry?

Ⓐ They want to take their time.

Ⓑ They do not want to wait in long lines.

Ⓒ They like to run a lot.

**3.** Which word rhymes with *twist*?

Ⓐ list

Ⓑ twirl

Ⓒ chips

**4.** What does the words *cling to* mean in this text?

Ⓐ hold on lightly

Ⓑ hold on for a while

Ⓒ hold on tightly

 

**NAME:** ______________________ **DATE:** ______________

**DIRECTIONS** Read the text. Answer the questions.

**SCORE**

1. ☺ 😐

2. ☺ 😐

3. ☺ 😐

4. ☺ 😐

____ / 4
Total

The lines are short, so they ride the roller coaster again. Then, they hurry to the log ride and get put in the two front seats. Guess what happens! When the log slides to the bottom, they get soaked!

**1.** Where do Nick and Fran go after the roller coaster?

Ⓐ the log ride
Ⓑ the front seats
Ⓒ the bottom

**2.** What kind of ride is the log ride?

Ⓐ a roller coaster
Ⓑ a water ride
Ⓒ a train ride

**3.** Which word is spelled correctly?

Ⓐ seets
Ⓑ seats
Ⓒ cets

**4.** What does *soaked* mean in this text?

Ⓐ damp
Ⓑ cold
Ⓒ wet

**NAME:** ______________________ **DATE:** ______________

# A New Ride

The amusement park has a new ride. It looks just like a pirate ship swinging high in the air. Fran and Nick watch the ship. It swings so high that it looks like it will go in a complete circle. They decide to try it next. They have a long wait, but the ride is worth it. They can see the entire park from the top when they are brave enough to look!

**NAME:** ____________________ **DATE:** ______________

**DIRECTIONS** Read "A New Ride." Answer the questions.

**SCORE**

1. Why do you think Fran and Nick watch the pirate ship?

   (A) They want to decide if they will ride it.

   (B) They want to take a break from rides.

   (C) They want to see if they are big enough to ride.

2. Which is true?

   (A) The ship goes upside down.

   (B) The ship swings back and forth.

   (C) The ship is not very high.

3. What do you think Fran and Nick thought about the ride?

   (A) that it was kind of scary

   (B) that it was too slow

   (C) that it was pretty easy

4. What would be a good name for this ride?

   (A) The Dragon

   (B) For Pirates Only!

   (C) Splashes

1. ☺ ☹
2. ☺ ☹
3. ☺ ☹
4. ☺ ☹

___ / 4
Total

**NAME:** ______________________ **DATE:** ______________

SCORE

___ / 4

**Reread** "A New Ride."

**Think about** the rides you know. Do you like to ride on them? Why or why not?

**Write about** a ride you like and why you like to ride it.

 

**NAME:** ______________________ **DATE:** ______________

**DIRECTIONS** Read the text. Answer the questions.

You may see lots of insects this summer. But you might not find this insect in your yard. The Hissing Cockroach comes from a large island near Africa. It is two to three inches long. It is as wide as a paper clip.

**1.** What do you know about this cockroach?

- (A) It is unusual.
- (B) You can find it in your yard.
- (C) It is only found in the summer.

**2.** What can you say about its size?

- (A) It is smaller than many insects.
- (B) It is bigger than many insects.
- (C) It is about the same size as many insects.

**3.** The word *insect* has two syllables: *in-sect*. Which word also has two syllables?

- (A) hose
- (B) horn
- (C) hammer

**4.** Which word means almost the same as *wide*?

- (A) funny
- (B) thick
- (C) shiny

**SCORE**

1. ☺ 😐

2. ☺ 😐

3. ☺ 😐

4. ☺ 😐

____ / 4 Total

**NAME:** ____________________ **DATE:** ____________

**DIRECTIONS** Read the text. Answer the questions.

SCORE

1. ☺ 😐

2. ☺ 😐

3. ☺ 😐

4. ☺ 😐

____ / 4
Total

Hissing Cockroaches hide on forest floors. They come out at night in search of fruit or plants to eat. The males have horns on their heads, and the females have bumps. This wingless cockroach is not a pest.

**1.** When do the wingless cockroaches come out to eat?

- (A) during the day
- (B) in the morning
- (C) at night

**2.** How can you tell a male from a female?

- (A) You can look at their color.
- (B) You can look at their heads.
- (C) You can look at their tummies.

**3.** Which word rhymes with *fruit*?

- (A) shoot
- (B) friend
- (C) cut

**4.** What does *wingless* mean in this text?

- (A) without horns
- (B) with one wing
- (C) without wings

 

NAME: ____________________ DATE: ____________

**DIRECTIONS** Read the text. Answer the questions.

SCORE

1. ☺ 😐

2. ☺ 😐

3. ☺ 😐

4. ☺ 😐

____ / 4
Total

The male cockroaches like to fight. They ram their horns into each other. They also hiss at each other. They push the air out through breathing holes in their bodies. This noise explains how the cockroach got its name.

**1.** How do the males fight?

Ⓐ ram and hiss

Ⓑ punch and hit

Ⓒ kick and spit

**2.** How do you know if a male cockroach is ready to fight?

Ⓐ It curls up.

Ⓑ It hisses.

Ⓒ It runs.

**3.** Which word is spelled correctly?

Ⓐ holes

Ⓑ hols

Ⓒ holez

**4.** What does the word *ram* mean in this text?

Ⓐ rub

Ⓑ hiss

Ⓒ push

**NAME:**______________________________ **DATE:**__________________

# Hissing Cockroaches

Some people like to raise these cockroaches. The female cockroach carries an egg case inside its body. It can have 50 babies at a time. Cockroaches can be kept in a dry fish tank with a lid. They will need clean bedding, fresh water, and food. They don't need special food. They can eat dog chow. For a treat, they like apple slices!

**NAME:** ______________________ **DATE:** ________________

**DIRECTIONS** Read "Hissing Cockroaches." Answer the questions.

**SCORE**

1. ☺ 😐
2. ☺ 😐
3. ☺ 😐
4. ☺ 😐

____ / 4 Total

**1.** Why would you need a lid on the dry fish tank?

Ⓐ The cockroaches could fly out.

Ⓑ The cockroaches could crawl out.

Ⓒ The cockroaches could swim out.

**2.** Why do you think people keep them as pets?

Ⓐ They are gross to watch.

Ⓑ They are fun to watch.

Ⓒ They are a lot of work.

**3.** Why do they need water and food?

Ⓐ so they stay healthy

Ⓑ so they stay in the tank

Ⓒ so they fight more

**4.** What is the main idea?

Ⓐ Cockroaches like to live in the forest.

Ⓑ Cockroaches are a pest.

Ⓒ It is not hard to have a cockroach as a pet.

**NAME:** ______________________ **DATE:** ______________

SCORE
___ / 4

**Reread** "Hissing Cockroaches."

**Think about** all the bugs you have seen. Which kind do you like to watch the most?

**Write about** your favorite bug. Tell why you like it.

 

# ANSWER KEY

## Week 1

**Day 1**
1. C
2. B
3. A
4. A

**Day 2**
1. B
2. A
3. A
4. C

**Day 3**
1. B
2. C
3. B
4. C

**Day 4**
1. B
2. A
3. B
4. A

**Day 5**
Responses will vary.

## Week 2

**Day 1**
1. B
2. A
3. B
4. C

**Day 2**
1. B
2. C
3. A
4. C

**Day 3**
1. C
2. B
3. B
4. A

**Day 4**
1. A
2. C
3. B
4. A

**Day 5**
Responses will vary.

## Week 3

**Day 1**
1. B
2. C
3. B
4. A

**Day 2**
1. A
2. B
3. C
4. B

**Day 3**
1. A
2. B
3. C
4. A

**Day 4**
1. C
2. A
3. B
4. A

**Day 5**
Responses will vary.

## Week 4

**Day 1**
1. C
2. B
3. B
4. A

**Day 2**
1. A
2. C
3. B
4. C

**Day 3**
1. C
2. A
3. B
4. A

**Day 4**
1. A
2. C
3. B
4. B

**Day 5**
Responses will vary.

## Week 5

**Day 1**
1. B
2. A
3. A
4. B

**Day 2**
1. C
2. B
3. A
4. C

**Day 3**
1. A
2. B
3. B
4. C

**Day 4**
1. B
2. A
3. A
4. B

**Day 5**
Responses will vary.

## Week 6

**Day 1**
1. C
2. B
3. A
4. A

# ANSWER KEY *(cont.)*

## Week 6 *(cont.)*

**Day 2**
1. A
2. B
3. C
4. A

**Day 3**
1. B
2. B
3. C
4. B

**Day 4**
1. B
2. A
3. C
4. B

**Day 5**
Responses will vary.

## Week 7

**Day 1**
1. B
2. C
3. A
4. B

**Day 2**
1. C
2. C
3. B
4. A

**Day 3**
1. B
2. C
3. A
4. A

**Day 4**
1. C
2. B
3. A
4. C

**Day 5**
Responses will vary.

## Week 8

**Day 1**
1. B
2. A
3. C
4. A

**Day 2**
1. B
2. B
3. A
4. C

**Day 3**
1. A
2. A
3. B
4. A

**Day 4**
1. A
2. C
3. B
4. C

**Day 5**
Responses will vary.

## Week 9

**Day 1**
1. A
2. A
3. C
4. C

**Day 2**
1. C
2. A
3. B
4. B

**Day 3**
1. B
2. B
3. C
4. A

**Day 4**
1. C
2. C
3. B
4. A

**Day 5**
Responses will vary.

## Week 10

**Day 1**
1. B
2. A
3. A
4. B

**Day 2**
1. B
2. C
3. A
4. C

**Day 3**
1. A
2. C
3. C
4. B

**Day 4**
1. B
2. A
3. A
4. C

**Day 5**
Responses will vary.

## Week 11

**Day 1**
1. B
2. A
3. C
4. A

**Day 2**
1. A
2. C
3. B
4. A

# ANSWER KEY *(cont.)*

## Week 11 *(cont.)*

**Day 3**
1. C
2. B
3. B
4. C

**Day 4**
1. A
2. B
3. C
4. B

**Day 5**
Responses will vary.

## Week 12

**Day 1**
1. C
2. A
3. C
4. A

**Day 2**
1. B
2. A
3. B
4. A

**Day 3**
1. B
2. C
3. A
4. A

**Day 4**
1. C
2. B
3. A
4. B

**Day 5**
Responses will vary.

## Week 13

**Day 1**
1. C
2. B
3. A
4. C

**Day 2**
1. B
2. A
3. B
4. B

**Day 3**
1. A
2. B
3. B
4. A

**Day 4**
1. C
2. A
3. C
4. A

**Day 5**
Responses will vary.

## Week 14

**Day 1**
1. C
2. B
3. A
4. B

**Day 2**
1. B
2. A
3. A
4. C

**Day 3**
1. A
2. A
3. C
4. C

**Day 4**
1. A
2. B
3. C
4. B

**Day 5**
Responses will vary.

## Week 15

**Day 1**
1. C
2. B
3. A
4. B

**Day 2**
1. B
2. A
3. B
4. C

**Day 3**
1. B
2. A
3. B
4. A

**Day 4**
1. A
2. C
3. B
4. A

**Day 5**
Responses will vary.

## Week 16

**Day 1**
1. B
2. C
3. A
4. A

**Day 2**
1. C
2. A
3. B
4. A

**Day 3**
1. A
2. A
3. C
4. B

# ANSWER KEY *(cont.)*

## Week 16 *(cont.)*

**Day 4**
1. C
2. A
3. B
4. C

**Day 5**
Responses will vary.

## Week 17

**Day 1**
1. B
2. C
3. A
4. A

**Day 2**
1. B
2. A
3. C
4. B

**Day 3**
1. A
2. B
3. B
4. C

**Day 4**
1. A
2. B
3. A
4. B

**Day 5**
Responses will vary.

## Week 18

**Day 1**
1. C
2. B
3. A
4. B

**Day 2**
1. C
2. B
3. B
4. A

**Day 3**
1. A
2. B
3. A
4. C

**Day 4**
1. A
2. B
3. A
4. A

**Day 5**
Responses will vary.

## Week 19

**Day 1**
1. B
2. A
3. C
4. C

**Day 2**
1. B
2. A
3. C
4. B

**Day 3**
1. A
2. B
3. B
4. C

**Day 4**
1. C
2. A
3. C
4. A

**Day 5**
Responses will vary.

## Week 20

**Day 1**
1. A
2. B
3. C
4. B

**Day 2**
1. B
2. A
3. C
4. A

**Day 3**
1. A
2. B
3. B
4. C

**Day 4**
1. C
2. B
3. B
4. A

**Day 5**
Responses will vary.

## Week 21

**Day 1**
1. A
2. B
3. B
4. A

**Day 2**
1. B
2. C
3. A
4. C

**Day 3**
1. B
2. B
3. A
4. C

**Day 4**
1. A
2. A
3. B
4. A

**Day 5**
Responses will vary.

# ANSWER KEY *(cont.)*

## Week 22

**Day 1**

1. B
2. C
3. A
4. B

**Day 2**

1. B
2. B
3. A
4. A

**Day 3**

1. B
2. B
3. C
4. A

**Day 4**

1. B
2. A
3. A
4. C

**Day 5**

Responses will vary.

## Week 23

**Day 1**

1. C
2. A
3. B
4. C

**Day 2**

1. C
2. B
3. A
4. B

**Day 3**

1. C
2. A
3. A
4. B

**Day 4**

1. B
2. B
3. C
4. B

**Day 5**

Responses will vary.

## Week 24

**Day 1**

1. A
2. C
3. B
4. B

**Day 2**

1. B
2. B
3. C
4. B

**Day 3**

1. B
2. C
3. B
4. A

**Day 4**

1. B
2. A
3. A
4. C

**Day 5**

Responses will vary.

## Week 25

**Day 1**

1. C
2. A
3. A
4. C

**Day 2**

1. A
2. A
3. C
4. B

**Day 3**

1. C
2. A
3. A
4. B

**Day 4**

1. A
2. B
3. C
4. B

**Day 5**

Responses will vary.

## Week 26

**Day 1**

1. C
2. A
3. C
4. B

**Day 2**

1. C
2. B
3. A
4. C

**Day 3**

1. A
2. B
3. C
4. B

**Day 4**

1. C
2. B
3. B
4. C

**Day 5**

Responses will vary.

# ANSWER KEY *(cont.)*

## Week 27

**Day 1**
1. C
2. A
3. C
4. B

**Day 2**
1. C
2. A
3. C
4. C

**Day 3**
1. B
2. A
3. C
4. A

**Day 4**
1. B
2. A
3. A
4. C

**Day 5**
Responses will vary.

## Week 28

**Day 1**
1. B
2. A
3. C
4. C

**Day 2**
1. C
2. A
3. A
4. B

**Day 3**
1. A
2. B
3. C
4. B

**Day 4**
1. B
2. B
3. C
4. A

**Day 5**
Responses will vary.

## Week 29

**Day 1**
1. C
2. B
3. A
4. A

**Day 2**
1. A
2. C
3. A
4. A

**Day 3**
1. C
2. A
3. A
4. C

**Day 4**
1. A
2. A
3. C
4. B

**Day 5**
Responses will vary.

## Week 30

**Day 1**
1. C
2. B
3. C
4. A

**Day 2**
1. C
2. B
3. B
4. C

**Day 3**
1. C
2. B
3. C
4. A

**Day 4**
1. A
2. B
3. B
4. A

**Day 5**
Responses will vary.

## Week 31

**Day 1**
1. B
2. C
3. C
4. C

**Day 2**
1. C
2. A
3. B
4. B

**Day 3**
1. C
2. B
3. B
4. C

**Day 4**
1. B
2. B
3. A
4. A

**Day 5**
Responses will vary.

# ANSWER KEY *(cont.)*

## Week 32

**Day 1**
1. B
2. C
3. C
4. A

**Day 2**
1. A
2. C
3. A
4. B

**Day 3**
1. B
2. A
3. A
4. C

**Day 4**
1. C
2. A
3. B
4. A

**Day 5**
Responses will vary.

## Week 33

**Day 1**
1. B
2. A
3. A
4. C

**Day 2**
1. C
2. C
3. B
4. B

**Day 3**
1. B
2. B
3. B
4. C

**Day 4**
1. B
2. A
3. C
4. A

**Day 5**
Responses will vary.

## Week 34

**Day 1**
1. B
2. A
3. C
4. A

**Day 2**
1. C
2. B
3. C
4. B

**Day 3**
1. C
2. A
3. B
4. A

**Day 4**
1. C
2. B
3. C
4. A

**Day 5**
Responses will vary.

## Week 35

**Day 1**
1. C
2. A
3. B
4. A

**Day 2**
1. A
2. B
3. A
4. C

**Day 3**
1. A
2. B
3. B
4. C

**Day 4**
1. A
2. B
3. A
4. B

**Day 5**
Responses will vary.

## Week 36

**Day 1**
1. A
2. B
3. C
4. B

**Day 2**
1. C
2. B
3. A
4. C

**Day 3**
1. A
2. B
3. A
4. C

**Day 4**
1. B
2. B
3. A
4. C

**Day 5**
Responses will vary.

# REFERENCES CITED


Marzano, Robert. 2010. When Practice Makes Perfect...Sense. *Educational Leadership* 68 (3): 81–83.

National Reading Panel. 2000. Report of the National Reading Panel. *Teaching Children to Read: An Evidence-Based Assessment of the Scientific Research Literature on Reading and its Implication for Reading Instruction* (NIH Publication No. 00-4769). Washington, DC: U.S. Government Printing Office.

Rasinski, Timothy V. 2003. *The Fluent Reader: Oral Reading Strategies for Building Word Recognition, Fluency, and Comprehension*. New York: Scholastic.

———. 2006. Fluency: An Oft-Neglected Goal of the Reading Program. In *Understanding and Implementing Reading First Initiatives*, ed. C. Cummins, 60–71. Newark, DE: International Reading Association.

Wolf, Maryanne. 2005. *What is Fluency? Fluency Development: As the Bird Learns to Fly*. Scholastic professional paper. New York: ReadAbout. http://teacher.scholastic.com/products/fluencyformula/pdfs/What_is_Fluency.pdf (accessed June 8, 2007).

# DIGITAL RESOURCES

## Accessing the Digital Resources

The digital resources can be downloaded by following these steps:

1. Go to **www.tcmpub.com/digital**
2. Sign in or create an account.
3. Click **Redeem Content** and enter the ISBN number, located on page 2 and the back cover, into the appropriate field on the website.
4. Respond to the prompts using the book to view your account and available digital content.
5. Choose the digital resources you would like to download. You can download all the files at once, or you can download a specific group of files.

ISBN:
9781425809225

**Please note:** Some files provided for download have large file sizes. Download times for these larger files will vary based on your download speed.

## CONTENTS OF THE DIGITAL RESOURCES

**Teacher Resources**

- Assessing Fluency
- Writing Rubric
- Practice Page Item Analysis Chart
- Student Item Analysis Chart

**Student Resources**

- Practice Pages

# NOTES